S
THE DESERT

SEEDS OF
THE DESERT

LIKE JESUS AT NAZARETH

by R. Voillaume

Prior General of the Little Brothers of Jesus

Translated and adapted by Willard Hill

ANTHONY CLARKE BOOKS

WHEATHAMPSTEAD · HERTFORDSHIRE

© 1972 Anthony Clarke Books, Wheathampstead, Hertfordshire.

Extracts from *Seeds of the Desert*, including passages hitherto unpublished, from *Au Coeur des Masses: La Vie religieuse des Petits Frères du Père de Foucauld*, Les Éditions du Cerf, 1953, Paris.

SBN: 85650 003 8

Made and Printed in Great Britain
by The Campfield Press, St. Albans.

FOREWORD

This little book has been drawn from a work published in France (*Au Coeur des Masses: La Vie religieuse des Petits Frères du Père de Foucauld*), which is known, in an abridged version, in English-speaking countries under the title of *Seeds of the Desert: The Legacy of Charles de Foucauld*.

As was pointed out in the foreword to that translation, "if the Little Brothers of Jesus—or the 'Little Brothers of Father de Foucauld,' as they are often called —began their existence in France, it was not because they were to be a French order. . . . The message of Charles de Foucauld . . . has nothing to do with frontiers. It is a call to Christians of our times everywhere to live the Gospel as it is."

The reception with which this message is in fact being met has encouraged us to believe that the time has come to help it to spread still more broadly. It is therefore with a view to meeting this possible need that this first series of selections from *Au Coeur des Masses* is being published in a paperback.

These extracts have been given the title "Like Jesus at Nazareth" because Father de Foucauld—or "Brother Charles of Jesus," as he wished to be known—in inaugurating, by his life and ideas, a new form of the religious life in the Church, envisaged his ideal in constant reference to the mystery of Nazareth—the mystery of the Word assuming the life of the "little people" who toil in the world and thus showing forth, as it were, from the start, something of the infinite respect, understanding and sensitiveness with which He meant to offer His love and His mercy to men, without forcing them. So it was, too, in this quite ordinary kind of existence, that the Son was "about His Father's business" (Luke 2, 49); for, having come into the world as the Saviour on the bidding of the Father, He was already walking the road that would lead him to the Cross.

Father de Foucauld not only embraced but lived both these sides of the mystery of Nazareth with all the fervour and consistency of an unfailing love for his "beloved Brother and Lord," Jesus, silently sharing in this way Our Lord's work of redemption. The religious life of his disciples is consequently so marked by the same tendencies that they could not be better described than as "contemplatives thrust straight into the world and the world's misery" (cf. Part II)—contemplatives, it may be added, whose desire it is to announce the Gospel "by their lives" and to "help to pay off the debt which the afflictions of Christ leave still to be paid, for the sake of His body, the Church" (Col. 1 : 24).

In short, as Father John LaFarge so aptly said in his preface to the American edition of *Seeds of the Desert*, the Little Brothers' work "would seem to spring from ... a firm confidence that God's grace will prompt and aid the willingness of very ordinary and seemingly indifferent people to learn to love God, if only God's love for them can be brought closer to their daily lives by the companionship and example of other men."

This is true of the Little Brothers' vocation, that is, of their place in society. Once again, however, the message which they have been chosen to further has no more to do with classes than with frontiers.

TABLE OF CONTENTS

I

Brother Charles of Jesus

and

The Mystery of Nazareth

". . . take the life of Nazareth in its simplicity and broadness as your objective in every way and in every connection . . . no special costume or habit—like Jesus at Nazareth . . . no enclosure—like Jesus at Nazareth . . . no isolated place of abode, but close by some village—like Jesus at Nazareth . . . not less than eight hours of work (manual or otherwise, but the former as far as possible) per day—like Jesus at Nazareth . . . neither large properties, nor large buildings, nor large expenditures, nor even large sums in alms, but real poverty in every respect—like Jesus at Nazareth. . . . Pray as Jesus prayed, pray as much as Jesus prayed; always make plenty of room for prayer . . . and, as He did, do plenty of manual work, for manual work does not mean time taken from prayer, but time given to prayer. . . . The life of Nazareth can be led anywhere at all; you must lead it wherever it will be most helpful to your neighbor."

(*Extract from one of Father de Foucauld's diary-notebooks, dated July 22, 1905*)

CHAPTER

1

BROTHER CHARLES
OF JESUS

Born in France in the second half of the last century; dying, assassinated, in the Sahara in 1916, Charles de Foucauld passed through this world at a period of history which, recent as it was, was very different from the one we are living in today. Yet, in his life and work, there is an authentic message for us from God, and his ideal of courageous Gospel simplicity is acting upon more and more young people of many nations and many races.

Though belonging to a family of the aristocracy with strong traditions and enviable records of chivalry, Charles de Foucauld had given up practicing his religion at a fairly early age. He even claimed to have lost his faith. Rationalism was the thing at the time. After his early schooling with the Jesuits, he attended the St. Cyr Military Academy. Here he finished among the lowest of his class, for he was leading a life of dissipation and laziness, and altogether behaving very badly. For some time after he had become a lieutenant and was seeing service, he carried his misbehavior to the point of living openly with a young woman whom he defiantly passed off as his wife, and when his superior officers finally ordered him to send her away, he refused point-blank, and resigned his commission. Everything seemed to show that Charles de Foucauld was cutting out for himself a life of brilliant uselessness, devoid of all ideals.

Actually, Charles de Foucauld was of a purposeful, single-minded and generous nature, made for greatness. Bored as he soon became with a life of wealth, society, and pleasure, he carried it for a time to almost fantastic extremes. Here is something he wrote, later on, about this phase of his life:

> I committed evil, but I neither liked it nor approved what I was doing. And You, Lord, would make me feel an emptiness, a despondency such as I have experienced at no other time but then. . . . It would come back every night when I found myself alone again in my flat. I continued to arrange my parties, but, once they would start, I would go through with them with infinite boredom and sickening disgust. . . .

His need to accomplish something, to give himself to something bigger than himself, was to lead Charles de Foucauld to undertake the exploration of Morocco. This happened around 1880. Morocco, at the time, was still a place of mystery where Europeans were not admitted. Dressed as a Moroccan Jew, claiming to be a rabbi from Central Europe, Charles de Foucauld travelled through the greater part of Morocco

for something like a year and a half, with a genuine
rabbi, called Mardoche, as his guide and counsellor.
The expedition was rife with adventure. De Foucauld
risked his life on more than one occasion and displayed not only true qualities of bravery, endurance,
and perseverance, but remarkable ability at scientific
observation as well.

On his return to France, he published the results
of his expedition in a weighty volume entitled *A
Reconnaissance in Morocco*, which immediately
ranked him among the great explorers and made him
known overnight. Fame lay at his door. But it was
not this that Charles de Foucauld wanted. He was
still unsatisfied. Through the faith of an entire people
of Moslems, he had glimpsed something of the greatness of God. His subsequent reading, a short period
of retirement and reflection, the example of his family
and, above all, a meeting with a saintly priest, Abbé
Huvelin, all helping, the faith of his childhood began
to revive. And one day, quite unexpectedly—for he
had simply called for a talk—he found himself on his
knees before Abbé Huvelin, went through a complete
confession, and was sent straight off to take Communion.

With his logical mind and strong-willed temperament, there were to be no half-measures for him. As
he wrote some time later, "The moment I realized
that God existed, I knew I could not do otherwise
than to live for Him alone."

To love, Charles de Foucauld considered, was to
wish to imitate. It therefore became his desire to live
like Jesus at Nazareth. So, first, he decided to enter

a Trappist monastery—the poorest of Trappist monasteries, Our Lady of the Snows, in a mountainous district in the southern part of France. Not long afterwards, however, he was asking to be transferred to a still poorer monastery which had recently been founded in the northern part of Syria; and his request was granted. Seven years he was to remain a Trappist, the most edifying and austere of Trappists. Yet his soul was still unsatisfied, for again he felt an irresistible urge for another kind of life. "I am not yet satisfied. I long for Nazareth."

Clearly, "Nazareth" meant to him, not just a hidden life lived in detachment from the world, a life of work behind the walls of a monastery, but a life amid the poor in the world, an actual status of life which would make him a man regarded and treated like one of the little people, one of the poor of this world.

Brother Charles's very special vocation was tested out by his superiors for several months and finally recognized as authentic. Whereupon he was released from his profession as a Trappist. With the approval of his spiritual director, he left for the Holy Land and arrived in Nazareth dressed like a beggar. Here he got work as a handyman and gardener at the convent of the Poor Clares, where he lived in a small wooden hut six feet square in a corner of the garden. He at last possessed what he had so long desired: to live like a poor man where Jesus Himself had lived a poor man.

Charles de Foucauld then spent two years of silence and prayer in the Holy Land. For hours at a stretch, he would remain on his knees, motionless, before the Blessed Sacrament, and whatever free time he might have from his work he would devote to meditating on the Scriptures and writing out his thoughts. Jesus present in the Eucharist, Jesus present in the Gospel: these two memorials of the Savior were the two poles around which his life revolved.

Brother Charles was convinced that he was one day to have Little Brothers with him. "Fraternities" was how he wished his monasteries to be called. The Little Brothers were to live grouped, as it were, around Jesus, like the Holy Family in Nazareth. As a great missionary ambition was growing more and more in his heart, an immense desire to bring the Gospel to people, and very particularly to the poorest and the most forsaken, he wanted his Little Brothers too to be apostles, by their entire lives.

And so it was that he entered upon a new phase of his life. Leaving Nazareth and the land of Jesus, he returned to France and became a priest. He had ceased rebelling against this idea, as he had when still a Trappist, because he had come to see that he could conciliate the exercise of the priestly function with his desire for littleness and poverty.

Now, there was not a single priest in Morocco and Father de Foucauld's exploration there had prepared him particularly well for such an abandoned territory. While waiting for an opportunity to get into the country, Father de Foucauld settled down at Beni-Abbes, an oasis situated in the Sahara to the east of Morocco, and built a mud 'fraternity' and a chapel.

Here he adopted the white tunic worn by the
Arabs of the desert, with a red cloth emblem—a heart
topped with a cross—sewed on the bosom of it. He
lived very poorly. He welcomed—better, gave himself
to—all: to the poor of the village, to the travellers
passing through, to the local slaves; even buying
some of the slaves and setting them free. (He would
send for money for the purpose either to his family
or to friends in France.) Each evening, he would explain a few passages of the Gospel to the poor people
who came to see him.

But the brothers he was hoping for did not appear,
and Morocco continued to be impenetrable. So finally
Father de Foucauld allowed himself to be prevailed
upon by his old classmate, General Laperrine, to consider moving still farther south, into the heart of the
desert, where the Touareg tribes live, still more forsaken than the people at Beni-Abbes.

. A thousand miles inside the Sahara, alone of his
race, the only Christian amid a very primitive people—this was how Father 'de Foucauld was now to
live.

The village of Tamanrasset, where he settled, is the
center of the Touareg country, the Hoggar, whence
the nomads radiate far and wide through the sur-
rounding mountains, with their hide tents and their
camels and their goat herds. Brother Charles
promptly had a hut built for himself here—a small
mud construction roofed in with palm trunks, just
like those of all the inhabitants. He immediately

started paying visits and inviting the people to come
to see him. He made himself the kind of friend at
whose door one may knock at any time of the day or
night. Since there was only one room in the hut, he
would have had no way, when at home, of avoiding
even the importunate, had he indeed wished to avoid
them; all anyone had to do was to open the door and
there he was, either working at his table or praying
before the altar. At Tamanrasset, Brother Charles was
a man devoured.

Nor was it merely a matter of practicing hospital-
ity, rendering service, caring for the sick. He gave
himself much more deeply to his Touaregs. He sought
to penetrate the secrets of their language, their traditions and their customs, in order really to understand
them. He spent an enormous amount of time writing
a Tamashek grammar and dictionary, and collecting
the tribal proverbs and poems. He had made it a matter of primary duty to enable himself to see into the
soul of the people, and it was because he loved them
that he wished to know them so thoroughly.

The plane on which Brother Charles succeeded in
establishing his relationships with the inhabitants of
the Hoggar was the plane of friendship—friendship
with a certain kind of equality, brought about by his
love.

Meanwhile, what of his plans for a foundation?
Brother Charles remained convinced that it was his
mission to work for the foundation of a double family
of Little Brothers and Little Sisters, but he knew now

that no disciples would come during his lifetime. "Jesus," he recorded, "wishes me to work for the establishment of this double family . . . in supplication, in self-immolation; by dying, by sanctifying myself, by loving Him, in short . . ." (January 10, 1905).

In fact, he had a presentiment that he would not live long. He had felt for some time that a certain kind of death awaited him. He wanted it so, and he made the following note one day: "Remember that you are to die a martyr, despoiled of everything, stretched out on the earth, naked, unrecognizable, covered with blood and wounds, killed with violence and in great pain. . . ."

God even asked him for the sacrifice of his one humble desire: to have at least one companion who could carry on the work after him. God refused to accede to that desire, as if to force Father de Foucauld to engender his sons and daughters by an ultimate act of blind faith—I mean, by believing that they would come despite all human appearances, like Abraham obeying God's command to sacrifice the son of the Promise. Charles de Foucauld was killed on December 1, 1916, by a band of Senoussis from the south of Tripolitania. Betrayed by one of his neighbors, dragged out of his house with ruthless force, he let them tie his hands behind his back as he knelt on the sands in front of his door, not uttering a single word—and a few minutes later, a young Touareg shot him through the head.

"If a grain of wheat falls into the ground and dies, then it yields rich fruit."

"Jesus wishes me to work for the establishment of this double family. . . ." It is nearly fifty years since Charles de Foucauld fell thus, there in the desert, leaving no one to succeed him. Today the "double family" of Little Brothers and Little Sisters he so longed for but never saw, numbers many hundreds of religious—not to mention the other groups of different sorts which now help to make up a constantly growing spiritual family with a highly diversified character.

Nor can we, his sons and daughters, read over these lines of his today without some feeling of awe and wonder. They are the "birth certificate," as it were, of all these Fraternities of ours, delivered long before these ever came to life. When the first disciples of Brother Charles began to appear, their founder was no longer there to receive them and point the way and present them to the Church. But what founder has ever planted deeper the seeds of fruit to come?

Lying at the roots of the Fraternities, there is, indeed, a treasure-hoard of renunciation, of silent self-abasement, of total self-effacement, a treasure-hoard buried away by Brother Charles against the day we should come to draw upon it for our lifeblood. In order to found in the end, he had to consent to what seemed the definitive impossibility of his cherished ideas, to renounce even the least of his many projects. Yet he surely engendered the Fraternities, in the extreme purity of his love for our Lord, through the sacrifice—the truly heroic sacrifice for a nature like his—of a most rightful desire, that of being given companions who could go on loving Jesus as he had loved Him himself.

No disciple of Brother Charles of Jesus must ever forget this hard and searching lesson, which meant renouncing all observable success, acquiescing to the apparent uselessness of an entire life, accepting failure in loving imitation of men's Savior, betrayed and crucified. For such is the "grain" from which Charles de Foucauld's Fraternities have sprung. No more must the Fraternities as such ever lose sight of the kind of "charter" under which they were originally founded or of the particular spiritual substance with which they were kneaded at the start.

2

THE MYSTERY OF NAZARETH IN THE LIFE OF BROTHER CHARLES OF JESUS

As from the time of his conversion, Brother Charles of Jesus discovered the *person* of Jesus, and gave himself to that Person once and for all. This personal relationship with a God, this friendship with the Word Incarnate at once so close and so distant, so familiar in His humanity and so transcendent in His divinity, this constant intimacy with his "beloved Brother and Lord Jesus," as he was fond of calling Him with an infinite reverence blended with a great tenderness—this friendship, then, was Charles de Foucauld's sole activating motive, what he was to live for passionately all the rest of his life.

There had come to him an irresistible urge to "put everything within the love of Jesus." A compelling need to imitate our Lord in his life thus not only turned all his outer activities, like his daily behavior, into such an imitation, but was the initial factor by which his vocation was to be determined. It was not enough, as I say, for him to adhere to Christ inwardly, to be united to Him with all the love in him, and to reproduce His virtues; he must also attain to complete conformity with Him *in his outer life*.[1]

Such is the logic of love that it carries with it, in the measure of its intensity, a need to be and do like the one one loves. This is a law of love, and it likewise applies to our love for our Lord. We must strive with all the weight of our charity for God for conformity with His Word Incarnate. Our imitation will vary only in its form, according to our individual vocations and the particular status or circumstances under which we live.

Father de Foucauld's form of imitation was peculiarly his own. His need was for imitating Jesus in His life at Nazareth. He felt no call whatever to any regular ministry, and the resulting decision with him, which, as a matter of fact, was already clearly in the making during his first retreats, was final.[2] For, from

---

[1] Every Christian is expected to be another Christ by spiritual imitation, but imitation through outward conformity with the way Christ lived is not essential to the perfect transformation of a soul in Christ. It may, however, become so for particular souls, in consequence of a particular and essentially individual vocation.

[2] "The Gospel proved to me that the 'first commandment' was for me to love God with all my heart, and that I must *put everything within that love*; and, as everybody knows, one of the effects of love is *imitation*. . . . I did not feel at all made for imitating Him in His public life and His preaching; I consequently knew I must imitate the hidden life of the poor and humble Workman of Nazareth . . ." (Letter to Henri de Castries, April 14, 1901).

the day of his conversion to the time of his death, this ideal stood out as the focus of all his aspirations, the point towards which his every act and his every step were directed.

Beginning upon the Holy Family's return after the flight into Egypt, the thirty years during which Jesus lived at Nazareth ended with forty days and forty nights in the wilderness, which thus appear at one and the same time as the prelude to His public life and the completion of His "hidden life," as the term customarily goes to qualify the Nazareth period. But what does this mean, exactly?

The term has often been used by authors of works of spirituality to designate a body of virtues, or dispositions of soul, the effect of which upon their possessor is to predispose him to live entirely within himself and apart from other men. Of this nature are the virtues of humility, poverty, obedience, and the love of recollection, silence, solitary prayer, self-effacement, obscurity and, in a certain manner—to use a word of which Father de Foucauld was particularly fond—"abjection." All of these no doubt had their place in the life led by our Lord at Nazareth; yet, emphasizing as they do an attitude of retirement from contact with men, they can only be said to have made up what one might call the "passive" side of it. It is likewise in this sense that "the hidden life" is often proposed as a model for the contemplative religious life.

Now, the life led by Jesus and His parents in their small town in Galilee was actually more complex than this, and it cannot properly be called just "hidden" in the spiritual sense just noted.

It is difficult—and, in fact, useless—for us to picture the psychology of the adolescent Jesus, man and God, a village artisan, rooted by His human nature in a race, a clan, and a family to the same degree as any Israelite of the time, and yet possessed, as God, of awareness of His divine personality, knowledge of His universal mission of redemption, and the ability to see into the world of souls. Besides, this interior life of the Son of God and the Savior, with all its redemptive value, was not, of course, that of the Nazareth period alone. What was proper to this period, on the other hand, was the kind of existence which Jesus embraced, though He knew He was God, knew He was the Mediator come among men, knew He was the bearer of a message to be delivered to the world. His soul burned with an immense and total love for His Father and all His brethren of the earth, and still, with intent, He kept silent. More still, He hid—perhaps even from His parents, from His mother, at least up to a point, and in any case completely from His fellow inhabitants—all the essential part of His inner life as the Christ, of His mission as the Redeemer. It is in this very precise sense that His life was really "hidden."

Just what all the reasons for this attitude may have been we shall never entirely succeed in understanding; we cannot help asking ourselves how Jesus could have refrained from letting the abundance of light that was in Him shed itself spontaneously upon those whom He was elbowing every day. But, during all the years at Nazareth, there was this manifest determination not to preach the Gospel, not to perform miracles, despite the incessantly renewed solicitations which the sight of the miseries and sufferings and griefs around Him could but be for Him at every turn. The Christ, the Word Incarnate, the Son of God remained in hiding, buried Himself as it were in the obscurity of the daily life of Jesus, son of Joseph. Nor was it by isolating Himself from people that the Christ remained thus concealed in Jesus. To have retired from the world and gone into solitude would have been to do something abnormal which would have attracted the attention of His fellow citizens. On the contrary, He hid His higher personality by mixing with His fellow citizens as much as He could, by losing Himself in their midst.

Jesus was *like everybody else*; the Gospel proves this indisputably. He kept His secret so well that not one of the inhabitants of the village, not one of His relatives—outside of Joseph and Mary—ever suspected at any moment that He might be different from other men. Or perhaps it would be better to say that, whatever the astonishment His behavior may have aroused, it was never enough to jeopardize His "disguise." The scandalized surprise displayed by the Galileans when He began to preach, and the lack of understanding of His mission on the part of members of His family, show this clearly.[3]

---

[3] See Mark 6:1-6; John 7:5.

It is indeed in this completeness of the incarnation, this total adaptation to, and utter burying-away in, the human environment, that the essence of the mystery of our Lord's life at Nazareth lies. The other aspects of it were but its concrete consequences, in that they served to characterize the *state in life* which He had chosen.

Our state in life is seldom the result of a free choice; in any case, the choice is never entirely free. It is influenced by too many factors over which we have no control. Who among us, for instance, has ever chosen his family, his race, his environment, his up-bringing, or even the religion in which he was raised? What, too, of the destiny of our persons? Is not the destiny which each of us has a mystery—a mystery of which God, when all is said and done, remains the sole ordainer? Jesus' state in life, on the contrary, was the result of a *sovereignly free choice*, and it therefore can but be regarded as a matter of peculiar importance. Here we have a fact unique of its kind: the Son of God *chose* His family, chose His mother, chose His race, chose the spot He was to be born in, chose His place in human society, His means of sub-sistence and His occupation. An absolutely free choice, an absolutely personal choice, it denotes a definite preference for the state thus selected. It also denotes a will to teach us something through this very choice.

Though the family into which Jesus was born was of royal blood, they were poor people, and they lived in a village of no particular importance. This did not mean misery, but the poverty of the worker. Neither did it mean the lowest rung of the social scale. In other words, the social rank and the manner of living embraced by Jesus were those of the majority—indeed, the great majority—of mankind; and He was thus able not only to hide Himself the better but, at the same time, to espouse the more ordinary, and therefore in a sense the most completely human, course of men's lives.

It would not be worth our while to try and picture just what the level of this existence was by comparison with the social differences existing today. The institutions of Jewish society at the time were too fundamentally different from ours for any such comparison to be possible. Jesus was an artisan or handicraftsman, and certainly had to undergo all the servitudes of His condition, such as bodily fatigue, exaggerated, and sometimes unfair, demands on the part of the customer, delays in the payment of the money owing to Him, days without work and the consequent worries, etc. All this helped to make up the ordinary run of His life for more than fifteen years; and to this must be added the family and neighborly relations which had to be kept up in accordance with local usage, and everything involved in the proper observance of the Sabbath and all the different feasts and customs. Jesus was undoubtedly scrupulously attentive to doing these things with His family, and anyone who knows how much more highly developed and exacting social relations are in Oriental societies than they are with us, can easily imagine what a wealth of them there must have been.

So much for the externals of our Lord's life at Nazareth, as the Gospel indicates them with a few rapid strokes.[4]

Father de Foucauld *discovered the different aspects of the mystery of Nazareth one after the other*, and not all at once, as his inner evolution enabled him to comprehend each in turn and put it into practice. It was the successive demands of his growth in charity that caused him to make these discoveries successively.

I

The first stage extends from Brother Charles's conversion to the end of his stay in the Holy Land. His desire to imitate Jesus was marked at this time by a need for concrete and almost minute realism, so strong as to make him wish to live on the very spots where Jesus had lived.

Devotion like this is doubtless imperfect love still in the making, and one cannot help thinking of some-

---

[4] Luke 1:39-56: the Visitation; Luke 2:21: the circumcision; Luke 2:22, 39: the Purification and the return journey to Nazareth; Luke 2:41: the annual pilgrimage to Jerusalem; Luke 2:43-45: the boy's disappearance; John 2:1-11: the wedding feast at Cana; John 2:14: Jesus at the Passover feast in Jerusalem; Luke 4:16 and Mark 1:21: Jesus' regular attendance at the synagogue; Luke 7:36: Jesus a frequent guest at meals; Mark 3:21: the opinion held of Jesus by His family; Mark 6:1-4: the astonishment aroused by His wisdom ("Is not this the carpenter . . . ?"), etc.

thing Jesus one day said to the Apostles: "It is better for you I should go away." But this was only a phase, just as some souls need at times to picture a setting as a prelude for their prayer. Moreover, Brother Charles came to recognize this very quickly, for, in one of his meditations, he emphasized that the mere fact of living in the Holy Land could in no way be compared with the spiritual good existing in any soul anywhere in the world.

Early in his conversion, Father de Foucauld likewise began viewing the mystery of the life of the Son of God in Galilee through an irresistible need *to seek abjection*. We find the expression constantly recurring in his writings. His whole idea of Jesus' life at Nazareth at this time was strongly influenced by this impulse—sometimes, in fact, a bit exaggeratedly. The attraction thus exercised over him was naturally accompanied by an equally strong desire for humility, obedience and poverty, mortification and penance.

The practice of these virtues was the surest way that Brother Charles could follow, for no genuine love can be built up from other bases. It was, indeed, because he managed to start practising these virtues from the beginning with complete generosity that he was able to love with such force and spontaneity. Humility, mortification, and poverty, and the habit of the retreat "disappropriated" him of himself, set him free to love. If a man is to give himself, he must first possess himself completely or, in other words, be in complete possession of his inner liberty and completely open and available. It is remarkable to note that for Brother Charles these virtues, by a sort of simultaneous reciprocal influence, were at once the preliminaries to and the fruit of his love.

But what I wish to go into more particularly at this point is Father de Foucauld's *passion for abjection*. We must dissociate his idea of the kind of life Jesus lived, assuming, as he said, "such a lowly place that nobody could ever have succeeded in taking it away from Him," from the desire for abjection which went so naturally with his way of loving. Jesus' life at Nazareth was actually a poor life, a hard and an infinitely humble life, but not a life of abjection. Brother Charles, on the other hand, needed abjection; and he was right.

How can one explain this? Where does this need of abjection, this need of humiliation, even of ignominy, which has welled up in the hearts of so many saints, come from? With all the saints, as with Charles de Foucauld, it is a consequence of a very great love for Jesus, a love beyond all measure. If one looks closely enough, one will see that this need exists in germ in any love—the tendency for any love is to prove itself to itself and tell itself in gratuitous outer acts for no other reason than love itself. If all human love contains a mystery which takes it beyond the rule of too reasonable reason, then what of divine love? Nor is this all. With the saints, the need of abjection is an effect of a complete conformity to the mystery of Jesus crucified. It is truly through a need for imitation—imitation in the stronger sense of assimilation, for, in each true Christian, Christ really lives over again Himself His mystery of suffering and abjection—that a Christian can find a mysterious joy and a mysterious peace in humiliation, obloquy, and blood-drawing disdain.

If Father de Foucauld was mistaken in imagining that there was any abjection in Jesus' life at Nazareth, he was most certainly right in following the instinct of his love when it enabled him to see, elsewhere in the life of our Lord, a veritable chasm of abjection. Anyone meditating properly on the Passion, can come to understand this. Setting up against the dignity of Christ's Person, the outrages, contempt and insults which were his lot on the Cross, one must certainly admit that there is a mystery hidden here, the *mystery of abjection*. This mystery is moreover seen to be the more formidable when one reflects that to be treated thus was Jesus' own choice, a choice the freer and the more conscious and deliberate as one can hardly say—even admitting that He could only efface the fault of mankind with a blood sacrifice—that this supreme sacrifice had necessarily to take place amid so much indignity. We can therefore but recognize in it all a mystery of love.

Can we henceforth let the mystery of Jesus live again in us without allowing it to establish this mystery of abjection in us also? If we really love Jesus, can we help wishing to prove our love to Him in the manner He Himself chose to prove His love to us? But, to be genuine, behavior of this sort must be not only a proportionate but a spontaneous expres-

sion of a love configuring us to Jesus crucified, which
has reached such a degree that it can be taken for
nothing other than the fruit of the activity in us of
the gifts of the Holy Spirit. It must remain what it
is, a manifestation of Divine Wisdom; and, as such,
the path will be different for each individual soul.
One's way of seeking abjection may easily be wrong,
constrained or premature; it does not then produce
perfect joy "in the Holy Spirit," but stops the more
often with a certain self-indulgence.

Care must be taken, then, to distinguish the *deliberate search for abjection*—an undertaking which,
again, can only be engaged upon under the motion of
the gifts of the Holy Spirit—from *love* of abjection
coupled with *desire* to suffer abjection in order to be
fully configured to Jesus crucified. This desire is in-
separable from true love for Jesus; it must spring from
our love and be proportionate to our love. At the very
least, we should be prepared—out of love for Jesus
scoffed at on the Cross—to accept the little humiliations and marks of disdain which are our lot, day in
and day out, with our fellow men. There can be
neither excess nor deviation in accepting this un-
sought for kind of abjection. Our faith can help us
to find in this acceptance the highest and purest kind
of joy—the perfect joy of experiencing something of
the bitter mystery of the Passion and of sharing in
the greatest and noblest labor which life can offer,
the ransoming of men.

There was as much abjection and contempt mixed
with Jesus' redeeming Passion as there was bleeding

and suffering; and we must not forget this, for we are often more afraid of having to bear humiliation than of having to shed blood. We must be honest enough with ourselves to recognize that we are not yet ready to seek abjection when, and if, we only have the desire of the honor of it.

I now come to another characteristic aspect of the frame of mind in which Father de Foucauld led his hidden life in his small wooden hut in the garden of the Poor Clares. I refer to his *faith in the real presence of Jesus in the Host*. In the conception he then had of the religious life as an imitation of Jesus' life at Nazareth, the Blessed Sacrament was to be the point around which everything was to center; the *presence of Jesus* was to configure the Fraternity to the house of the Holy Family. Concentrated as it was in this fervent cult of Jesus' presence in the Host, his piety contained in germ a completely Eucharistic life. Meanwhile the beloved presence of Jesus was not only the starting-point of his prayer life, it was in this attitude that he always prayed.

Such were the characteristic features of Brother Charles's spiritual countenance during his years of retreat in the Holy Land. So far, he had grasped, and lived, the life of Jesus at Nazereth almost exclusively from its "hidden" side, in the sense in which the "hidden life" was commonly thought of at the time, at least in France. In a way, he had given that idea of it a harsher note by picturing the Holy Family as living practically in retirement from the world around them and in almost continual silence and individual isolation. By doing so, however, he was able to settle his love of God at a level where it could resist all storms and whence it could develop with complete freedom and run no risk of deviating; and this is also an important point for us to note in connection with this first period.

In deciding to make of his entire life an imitation of Jesus' life, he placed it once for all in the line of Christ-centered contemplation. Everything must be, everything was, for Jesus. The life of the Little Brother must also, from the start, be oriented in this direction; for why have we determined to live a life of prayer and work and charity, if it is not for love of Christ and in order to achieve friendship with Him to the full? Like Father de Foucauld's, our charity must always be but an overflowing of the divine love —Jesus radiating Himself to others through us; never a too human enthusiasm for devoting ourselves to the service of others.

Let us have the courage to embrace as manfully as did Father de Foucauld all this work of "self-disappropriation" I have mentioned, which can only be accomplished through humility, obedience, mortification, poverty and this love of abjection which I have now, I hope, placed in its proper light. People at the present time are perhaps too inclined to minimize the importance of these basic virtues. Failure to place oneself in a state of complete availability—the fruit of the right kind of humility and of virile mortification—

is too often why, despite the greatest generosity, a soul either gets but a short distance in the practice of love or runs into some brutal temptation after a promising start. This, in a word, is building on sand rather than actually participating in the life of Christ. The life of Christ contains a mystery of death; and we have been associated with that mystery by our Baptism. Life comes out of death.

Settle your eucharistic prayer, too, on the solid foundation of a hardy, clear-minded faith in the real presence of Jesus. Be brave about it, because your faith, as it grows, will have to be purified of many of its present ingredients which are nothing but feeling. Its growth will take place more especially in prayer, and you can facilitate it by setting your faith, from the start, well in the pure light of the Divine Word.

II

The second period in the spiritual life of Father de Foucauld runs from his acceptance of the idea of the priesthood to the end of his stay at Beni-Abbes. His evolution during this period denotes a broadened conception of the life of Nazareth.

The Savior's *hidden redemptive activity at Nazareth* echoes more and more strongly in him; his soul is more and more eager for prayer and self-immolation for the salvation of all mankind.

The form this disposition finally takes is that of devotion to the Sacred Heart. One might almost say that the "Hermit of Beni-Abbes," as Brother Charles had now become, became haunted by concern over the salvation of souls.

As time goes on, he gives more and more time *to exercising charity—and very great charity—towards his neighbor*. Less and less is there any question of charity exercised behind the walls of a monastery alone, but rather of a whole *life of charity in direct contact with the world outside*. Father de Foucauld has been deeply struck by the idea that love of God and love of one's brothers not only go together but are, in fact, one and the same. He breaks his enclosure, alters his schedule completely, deliberately seeks contacts with all in the vicinity—Arabs, Negroes, and Europeans alike, while persisting in his desire to undertake no regular ministry or preaching or organized works. All this he views as falling within the framework of "Nazareth" and the mystery of the Visitation.* The development of the love of God going on in him, in other words, forces him, as it were, to discover— and so to live—this new aspect of the mystery of Nazareth, the contacts which Jesus and His parents must have had with their neighbors and the other people in the town.

III

Father de Foucauld's years at Beni-Abbes may be considered as a period of transition. It

---

* The Blessed Virgin, in the mystery of the Visitation, is the patron of the Fraternities.

was there that the gradual transformation took
place in him from an ideal of the religious life up till
then too narrowly defined by a Rule, too dependent
upon a frame, to an imitation of our Lord which was
to become constantly closer, constantly truer and, by
this very fact, much more submissive to the demands
of love for his neighbor, as well indeed as to the
knocks and jolts necessarily occurring in a life henceforth resolutely placed in immediate contact with his
fellow men. The wall he had begun to build around
his projected enclosure was finished off with a mere
row of white pebbles—until such time as the wide-
open hut at Tamanrasset should completely symbol-
ize the difference. But, for all that, the eyes of his
soul were continually fixed upon Jesus in infinite admiration and infinite worship.

While revealing no new fundamental factors, the
last years at Tamanrasset witnessed both the full development of Father de Foucauld's charity and the
complete possession of his vocation. His final conception of the life of Nazareth likewise no doubt worked
itself out in actual practice rather than through the
formulation of principles: a life free of outward con-
straints, *deliberately mixed with the lives of the
Touareg people*, and involving contacts quite openly
sought outside the Fraternity through visits, tramps
and prolonged tours. He likewise devoted a great deal
of effort to acquiring as thorough a knowledge as possible of everything concerning the language, the folk-
lore, and the customs of the inhabitants. In short, it
would be no exaggeration to say that Father de

Foucauld not only loved these people with a tremendous fraternal love, but adapted himself to them with disinterested, or better, "scientific" intellectual inflexibility and the greatest care to know and understand them completely.

Everything Father de Foucauld could do to make himself a part of the Ahaggar country he did, because it was "with his life" that he felt called to "cry the Gospel" and to preach in silence by practising the evangelical virtues. This, then, was why Father de Foucauld wished to mix so closely with the population and to be content with nothing less. His daily life, his whole way of living, down to his dwelling itself, were to help to make him one of them, as well as "little" and easy to approach.

But there would seem to have been something more still to Brother Charles's vocation than this mission of silent witness-bearing. In a letter written in May, 1911, he said that the Little Brothers might engage in apostolic work, but that any work they did of this character should be confined to preparing the way for the missionaries who would come later and establish the Church as an organized body. Again, he concerned himself with whatever might be of service to his neighbors or help to better the lives of the people. His interest extended to various aspects of the equipment and organization of the Touareg territory, such as the laying of practicable trails, the introduction of the first motor cars and the proper operation of the official administration. He completely gave himself to these people, not only spiritually, but humanly; for he well knew how intimately the Christian life is bound up with the whole context of human life. He made himself one of the people—a brother and a friend; humbly—never considering himself as in any way superior to them; and without ever allowing himself to feel or act or appear differently, he did everything he could to show them thus what the Gospel meant. There was, of course, something new in his way of preaching the Gospel "with his life."

Meanwhile, his devotion to the Holy Eucharist underwent a rather deep change in its expression. Going to settle in the heart of the Hoggar had meant sacrificing for several months the daily celebration of the Holy Sacrifice to the exercise of a higher charity, but this he had not hesitated to do—no more than he did being deprived of keeping the Blessed Sacrament in his tabernacle during the first six years of his stay at Tamanrasset. In the result, there came about a sort of purification in his eucharistic devotion, and the whole eucharistic side of his life was then more integrated in his love for Jesus. Henceforth, his approach to his love for his Touaregs was as one of the facets of the *single* charity uniting him to Christ. His devotion to the Eucharist itself he could no longer have thought of outside the very line of this living of charity, now simplified and unified in its supreme principle. The significance of this as showing the maturity to which his spirituality had now attained, is obvious.

His death, too, was the visible consummation, permitted by God, of an unvarying disposition that had constantly been in his soul: to save other souls by the

gift of his own being to God. The end he was allowed
to have was the seal; the way he met it was the ultimate proof of this, his greatest desire: to save as Jesus
had saved, to be a "savior with Jesus."

As Father de Foucauld's life unfolds before one's
eyes, then, one discovers all the different aspects of
the mystery of Nazareth as I have attempted to define it. First, there was the deep and solid hidden
life of *humility, poverty, prayer,* and *mortification*—
both the condition of, and the fruit of, his lasting attachment to Jesus. Secondly, there was the ardent
and constant desire *to cooperate in the Savior's work
of redemption* through prayer and the immolation of
his whole being in love, for friendship here always
leads to as complete a sharing as possible of the same
concerns and the same destiny; and this desire expressed itself very particularly through his *devotion
to the Blessed Sacrament.* Thirdly, there was the actual practising of love for mankind in friendly contacts and simple, human relationships with all, "such
as the Holy Family must have had at Nazareth." This
was his way of bringing the Gospel to those who did
not know it—"preaching it by example rather than by
word, by living it rather than by expounding it."

One aspect only of his ideal was he unsuccessful
in achieving, and that was to earn his living with
manual toil. He was prevented from doing so by the
circumstances prevailing in the places in which he
lived, as also by the fact of his living alone and, like-

wise, having to devote so much time to acquiring a foreign tongue.

Taken as a whole, the story of Father de Foucauld may be said to represent the achievement of an original ideal constantly and perseveringly pursued throughout the free development of a very individual life. This is the ideal which he held out to his foundations; and all that remained to be done, after his death, was to give it adequate adaptation in practice.

CHAPTER

3

"NAZARETH" AS A FORM
OF THE RELIGIOUS LIFE

The originality of Father de Foucauld's life may tend to hide for some the true nature of his vocation. He always said himself that it was to imitate the life of Jesus at Nazareth, but even if we did not know this, it would, I think, be clear to anyone really familiar with his history. For, from the day of his conversion to the time of his death, this ideal stands out as the focus of all his aspirations, the point towards which his every act and his every step were directed. I believe it will be equally clear that it was part of his vocation to make imitation of the mystery of Nazareth a veritable form of the religious life.

At first sight, there would seem to be nothing particularly new or original about this latter ambition. A whole current of authentic religious life has long been feeding upon the "spirituality of Nazareth." But one senses unmistakably—through the example of his life still more than through his writings, and despite the fact of his having lived out his life alone—that the religious ideal brought us by the "brother of the Touaregs" is something really new, though—and perhaps partly because—it was not to fructify until after his death.

The objection has been made to us more than once that a spirituality too closely centered upon the life at Nazareth would inevitably be narrow and incomplete. "Nazareth," they have said, was after all only one phase in Jesus' life and, long as it may have lasted, simply a period of preparation for His mission or a period of silent waiting until the moment fixed by the Father should come for Him to begin the work of the redemption. Why, then, confine oneself to this single aspect of Christ's example?

If certain insufficiently enlightened souls have sometimes failed to avoid the risks connected with devotion of a kind in which the mystery of Jesus is not included in its entirety, one can hardly put the blame for this on Father de Foucauld. To be certain of this, one only needs to read his meditations on the Gospel, on the one hand, and, on the other, to observe how he was little by little configured to Christ in the depths of his soul—not to the Workman of Nazareth alone, but to His errant life in search of the most lost of the lost sheep as well and, above all, to His agony on the Cross. It nevertheless remains that the mystery of the poor workman living in obscurity at Nazareth exercised a determining influence on Father de Foucauld's choice of the *status* he was to have, as well as on his plans for the religious congregation which he started thinking about at the very beginning. The inspiration he drew from "Nazareth" resulted in a *new outward form* for that life, his *spirituality* meanwhile taking its sustenance from the whole mystery of Jesus as he came upon its different aspects in the Gospel.

There are two particular features which seem to me to have been intrinsic to Brother Charles's manner of picturing the ideal religious life, two features which were to stand out little by little from the countless aspirations crowding into his soul, and which, little as he may have realized their full importance at the beginning, nevertheless contained the germ of a veritable renewal of the religious life.

The first of these made its appearance when he was still "Frère Alberic" at the Trappist Monastery at Akbes and went one day to pay a visit to a family of very poor working people in the neighboring village. The shock he received on seeing how these people lived by comparison with life at the monastery, simple and hard as this was, he recorded thus on his return: "Oh, the difference between these buildings of ours and that poor working man's house! It makes me long for Nazareth." From then on, "Nazareth" was to embody his ideal for the religious life, and this was to comprise the hard toil, the low scale of living, the meager housing and the insecurity of a family of workers.

But the question may be asked whether, in one's desire thus to attain religious perfection in the status in which the majority of mankind lives, one is not confusing somewhat the religious status and the normal situation of any Christian pursuing holiness in the world. The nature of Christian perfection is the same for all who have been baptized, whether laymen or religious, and the religious life is definable simply as a particular body of means to that end. Father de Foucauld himself emphasized that the ideal model for a layman to follow was the mystery of Nazareth. Yet it was the life at Nazareth and no other that he felt himself impelled to choose as a religious.

The second original feature of Brother Charles's ideal was to accentuate still further this unprecedented approach to the religious status. It would doubtless have been possible to restrict imitation of the life at Nazareth to a framework (withdrawal from society, enclosure, silence, etc.) which would have left it a traditional monastic cast, and Brother Charles indeed tried to see things that way for some time. But the inner pressure of his vocation was too strong; he was soon to abandon all idea of separations and live in direct contact with the people around him, a contact, moreover, made constantly closer by his growing charity and the need he therefore felt of expressing it more and more with the familiarity of simple, fraternal friendship. This gift of self, this constant availability were, then, the fruits of love and a great desire to bring these people the living presence of Christ. Nor should one hesitate to recognize here the apostolic spirit in the broadest sense of the term, provided one has fully grasped not only the particular nature of this kind of apostolate, but also that of the means it involved to the exclusion of all others. Merely being present was one of these, but there were also, as I say, the brotherly friendship, the gift of self, the intimate conversations, the testimony of the way he lived—in a word, whatever love could counsel a man of poverty in order to make his Lord known and loved by those around him.

Again, the objection has been made that if observances are done away with, or practically so, and, more particularly still, if there is not at least some minimal separation from the outside world, there can be little use talking about any real religious life, as what would be left would merely be tantamount to the life of Christian laymen in the world. Two different problems are thus raised: first, whether minimal separation and observances are really essential factors in the religious life as such, and, secondly, whether the religious state is superior to that of the layman or not.

Surely, it is one of the most important achievements of contemporary Christianity to have awakened consciousness of the fact that sanctity, total sanctity, is attainable in everyday life. Due to the rapid changes in general conditions which began towards the beginning of the century and the tragic upheavals which ensued, the great majority of people living the ordinary life of the world suddenly found themselves faced with an almost relentlessly hard and precarious existence, and this has been a challenge to Christians to get beyond themselves—often not without a certain heroism. At the same time, the Church was confronted in certain countries with the problem of winning back the de-Christianized masses of the people and, with many of the laity belonging to Catholic Action movements, this has helped to develop an active charity and an understanding of social facts and of the necessity of providing fraternal assistance, which the difficulties encountered in the daily struggle have only made the deeper.

On the other hand, a fairly large number of religious communities have remained unaffected by these conditions, as if sheltered from the changes going on outside—though quite involuntarily on their part. Very few religious in their monasteries and convents have been called upon to lead anything like a hard, let alone a heroic, life; rather have they been preserved from the harshness of life today by the very rhythm of their existence. It would be difficult to admit that this has been privilege, from the standpoint of the life of the Gospel.

Comparisons of this kind have had some share in the falling-off in respect for the religious status. The rapid evolution of people's minds today ought to have been met with a certain adaptation of religious observances and means to perfection to the new needs. This adaptation has not taken place as it should have, and it would seem as if the very slow change occurring in certain sides of the religious life had been considerably outdistanced by changes in the modern world.

Thus various deficiencies, which are sometimes real and sometimes only apparent, are partially responsible for the severity with which people today often regard the cloister; they do not, however, by any means justify all their statements, for these often spring from mistaken or inadequate ideas as regards our relationships with God.

There are two particular sides of the religious life which are especially badly understood nowadays: the *necessity of discipline and asceticism* not having as their direct aim or immediate purpose a tangible improvement in human values or observable results in the sphere of the apostolate, and the *value of consecrating one's life to God alone* outside any charitable activity or service to others.

At the root of this lack of comprehension, there is a reaction against the Jansenist, or, if you prefer, Puritan conception of man: people have difficulty in admitting original sin and the flaws and injuries with which it has left human nature. Original sin is hardly ever mentioned any more, and the idea of asceticism is only acceptable when presented for what it can do for people by augmenting their capacities. The significance of penitence and mortification is thus no longer perceptible; certain sacrifices that go with the vows of poverty and obedience are no longer understandable, and celibacy consecrated by vows no longer excites the same respect.

In addition, consciousness of the urgency of making society over on new bases and of winning back to Christ a world gone pagan to the marrow of its

bones, has caused the greater part of Christian thinking to crystallize around productive social activities
and efficiency of effort in human charity. An enrich-
ment has indubitably thus been brought about, but
it has had its unhappy counterpart in an impoverish-
ment of *feeling for the sacred*. The intrinsic value of
separating oneself off for the sake of God is contested;
likewise, sometimes, the very legitimacy of an existence consecrated so completely to God as to entail
withdrawing from all human activity. The tendency
is to judge the spiritual value of an action by what
that action is capable of producing in the way of results in social activity and service to one's neighbor.
This is an error, and this error explains why people
no longer properly appreciate the religious value of
the vow consecrating men and women to God.

We must therefore assert—in line with the position
unvaryingly held by the Church since the first centuries—that there is no question but that consecration
to God by the three vows is superior to the ordinary
Christian status. In making this assertion, we automatically make likewise the assertion, not only of the
legitimacy, but of the superiority *per se* of the *essential* separations—which must, first of all, be inner and
spiritual—involved in the observance of the vows,
in particular that of chastity. As for the question
whether separation, even when reduced to a minimum, is compatible with the kind of life, in intimate
contact with people and with everything it entails
in the way of instability, uncertainty of the morrow,
daily cares and daily toil, which Father de Foucauld

dreamed of from the time he left the Trappist monastery, I think we may answer in the affirmative.

The essential factor in the religious status, the thing which defines and distinguishes it as such, is the *spiritual reality* of the promise one makes to God, with the public acceptance of the Church, to live in a state of chastity, poverty, and obedience. Separations are, of course, entailed here; they can, however, be obtained under the most varied and different circumstances. A second factor, which, though secondary and non-essential in itself, may well be indispensable to some, is met with in the current conception of the religious status, and consists in a body of arrangements—enclosure, regulated silence, various forms of physical separations, and prescriptions concerning the organization of the community life—looking to the observance of the three vows in practice. These are but means as regards the actual practising of the evangelical counsels. It is consequently possible to conceive of a true religious life making use of these different means to a lesser degree, provided it offers a sure road to perfection in charity through the practice of poverty, chastity, and obedience. Such a road has been opened up for us by Father de Foucauld. It lies in sharing the lot of the workers and the other poor, with all the consequences involved, and being a living presence of Christ among them.

Here, then, is a new type of religious life, where less attention is paid to sheltering oneself off from risks with separations, or to being helped by observances superimposed upon one's daily occupations, than to ordering one's entire life into a single move-ment of charity for Christ and men, and learning to make use of the very difficulties attendant upon such a life as so many means to self-dispossession and the very concrete realization of one's profession of the three vows.

Those who are inclined to question the viability of this kind of religious life need only consult the pontifical documents in which Pope Pius XII gives solemn recognition to the form of life offered by the Secular Institutes as a canonical state of perfection and, in so doing, asserts in a manner which leaves no room for doubt, that the perfection of the evangelical counsels can be reached by a path which, at first sight, may seem opposed to the one hitherto followed by religious Congregations. By emphasizing that which is essential to the state of perfection with such fresh clarity and precision, these documents far ex-ceed by their importance their immediate object, and open up the way for a renewal of the conception of the religious life itself.

"To lead at all times and in all places a life of true perfection, to embrace such a life in cases where the canonical religious life would be either impossible or insufficiently adapted, to re-Christianize families, professions and civilian society with intensity through immediate and daily contact with a life fully and completely consecrated to one's sanctification. . ." (Apostolic Constitution, Provida Mater Ecclesia).

"Nothing must be retrenched from the complete profession of Christian perfection, solidly based upon the evangelical counsels and truly religious as regards its substance, but that perfection must be achieved and professed in the world; it must consequently be adapted to secular life in all things which are licit and compatible with the obligations and works of that perfection.

"The entire life of the members of the Secular Institutes, dedicated to God for the practice of perfection, must be converted into an apostleship. . . . This apostleship of the Secular Institutes must be exercised not only in the world, but likewise by the means of the world, so to speak, and consequently in professions, activities, forms, and in places and under circumstances corresponding to this secular condition" (Motu Proprio, *Primo feliciter*).[1]

Slightly transposed, these lines would be a perfect definition of Father de Foucauld's spirituality in its most essential features.[2] The two ideas which I

---

[1] Having been unsuccessful in obtaining any official English translation of the pontifical documents quoted above, the translator has been obliged to supply these renderings himself, working from the French texts published by "Documentation Catholique" (t. XLIV, col. 577 and t. LXV, col. 1089). *Translator's note.*

[2] It should at the same time be recalled here that Secular Institutes differ from religious Congregations, and therefore from the Fraternity of the Little Brothers, in two essential ways: firstly, while members undertake, by vow or promise, to observe poverty, chastity, and obedience, this undertaking is not considered by the Church as a public profession; secondly, members do not lead a common life, at least as a rule.

stressed above are both here: first, the will to practise
the three vows in an ordinary life, working at almost
any kind of work; then the need to be 'saviors' with
Jesus. This latter is the very reason for our Fraternities being buried away, as it were, in the heart of
mankind; and it is likewise the thing that justifies the
choice of such a vocation despite its risks. When one
stops to recall how Father de Foucauld's mind and
heart were tortured over men's salvation—"For the
spreading of the Gospel, I am ready to go to the ends
of the Earth and I am likewise ready to live till the
Day of Judgment"—that this was what made him
push farther and farther into the desert so as to reach
the most forsaken of the native tribes, what made him
spend so many hours not only in adoration, before the
Host, of the world's Savior but studying the language
and holding innumerable apparently useless conversations; that this was why he gave himself in such disinterested, and often quite fruitless, friendship—when
one realizes all this one can but admit that his life
could not be better described than by saying that it
was "entirely converted into an apostleship." It was
because his life itself was thus "entirely converted"
that there was no need for him to have recourse to
other means—those, I mean, which are usually associated with the commonly accepted idea of the apostolate.

You Little Brothers must therefore seek the perfection of love not only in contact with men, but
with such contact as a means to it, or, to use the

words of the pontifical document again, "not only in the world, but . . . by the means of the world."

Here is what takes the place of observances with us. If, in your lives of hard work, there were too frequent exercises or other moments of escape (though a harmonious use must, of course, be made of these with the appropriate rhythm), you would not succeed in consecrating the whole of them to God so well as you will by making the most of all the opportunities for abnegation, and meeting all the demands of charity, which your days will bring you almost at every turn. Your insecurity in your poor men's lodgings will help you to learn the joy of detachment from things material; the proletarian unsteadiness of your work, the fatigue of your everyday goings and comings and your travels will help you to learn to carry through with your renunciation of your restlessness and your self-interest. Your falls, experience of your weakness will not stop you, either; for, over and beyond it all, you will learn to seek the Lord's mercy, the source of the divine life. Finding yourselves, as you often will, unable to keep any time for yourselves, because people poorer than you will be taking possession of your very existence, will help to lead you to the inner peace of perfect poverty. You must nevertheless constantly have the same desire as Jesus to go apart by night and pray, and you must grasp every chance of satisfying that desire.

If a road like this has been formally recognized as a way to perfection for the Secular Institutes without

the life in common, must this not be still more the
case with us who possess the additional advantage of
the strength of our Fraternity life? If, again, the
Church recognizes the possibility of people leading
a life of poverty, chastity and obedience in the world,
whatever their profession and whatever their status,
this can but obtain even more in the particularly
humble, particularly poor kind of life voluntarily
chosen by the Little Brothers.

An objection sometimes made with regard to our
vocation is that the material conditions under which
the industrial worker has to work preclude any genuine religious life. But how is it that so simple a thing
as adopting a skill or a trade because one wishes to be
like the innumerable wage-earners in the world today;
how is it, I say, that such a gesture, which has been
made out of sheer love by so many saints through the
centuries since our Lord Himself lived as a manual
worker, raises such questions that the idea of integrat-
ing work with the religious life has become almost
inconceivable outside the very limited framework
of the closed, and often very special, economy of a
monastery? Has the life of the modern workman then
become such as to be incapable of supplying a basis
on which to build an authentic religious life?

If this had to be admitted, it would be something
tragically serious; for the mass of people condemned
to the servitude of the conditions under which the
worker often lives is growing every day, and the opposition, the painful, the unacceptable opposition

reigning in so many different countries between the people and the Church of Jesus would then become an accepted fact.

If religious, impelled by the call of Jesus and sustained by everything the training and framework of the religious life can bring them, can find no means of striving towards the perfection of love in toiling like the workers, what will be the case with the workers themselves? And there are hundreds of millions of men in these circumstances!

Not one among us can entertain any doubt on the point. Nor is there any separating, in our line of vision, Jesus working at Nazareth and the immense mass of workers plodding under the weight of a daily drudgery too often made inhuman by other men's wills or some blind machine. We firmly believe that we can share their lot with all the love in us, and that we can carry them Jesus through our lives; we also trust that it will be made possible for them to attach themselves, through the Fraternities, to the Church. If we are to achieve this purpose, we must in all ways remain men of the Church, yet make ourselves true brothers to the workers both in heart and in lot.

Among the obstacles which would supposedly prevent us from making a life entirely consecrated to God out of a worker's life, are the *fatigue* involved, as ill disposing the mind for prayer, and the *limited time* left for prayer by the schedule of working hours. This is the kind of objection most often put forward by religious of the contemplative Orders,

and I quite understand their point of view, because
the trend of their religious life is all in the direction
of separation, solitude and silence. Their souls are
thus properly predisposed for contemplative prayer
and made receptive to the particular action of the
gifts of the Holy Spirit which is meant to go with
that *form of prayer*. This latter is more especially
a peaceful contemplation of the divine beauty and
truth under the light of love. It does not therefore
cover the whole ground of prayer; nor does it appear
to be the kind of prayer which Jesus wishes from the
Little Brothers, at least not as a rule. The kind of
prayer to which we are specially committed by the
character of our life is what I might call "redemptive
prayer" and this, different as it may be in form from
that of the cloistered religious, is nevertheless true
and authentic prayer. Not only does it not take place
with us within the same framework, it must be exercised under conditions which would seem to be
the exact opposite to theirs. In other words, it more
than often has to be offered in the fatigue and the
pain and the difficulties of a life of poverty, which
can also be a very busy one.

This self-injection of ours in suffering humankind
is indicative enough of the way our prayer should
come, and there should be no question of any mixing
of forms in this respect. For the Carthusian or the
Trappist, it is a duty to make their prayer a thing
apart so it may be pure contemplation; the Little
Brother, on the other hand, must carefully avoid acquiring the habit of separating his prayer from the

share of human anguish which he bears within him. Rather must he take into his soul the prayer of mankind harnessed to its daily drudgery. Let it therefore be no surprise to you, Little Brothers, to find that your prayer, more often than not, must take the form of a painful straining, or an empty wait in darkness, or a thirst stretching up towards the Savior to be quenched, with an awareness of your insufficiency and weakness at times so acute as to be an affliction to you. I do not believe that your vocation admits normally of your being given any form of prayer that you could stop and rest in. Your lot is bound up—and you have also willed it so—with the lot of your fellow men moving painfully towards the light. By exercising prayer of pure faith, you can secure for them that minimum of faith which they must needs have in order to turn their lives in God's direction; by the effort of hope by which your hearts at certain moments will be heavily lifted up to Jesus, you can succor those who despair; by a love which will be more of an unsated hunger to find Jesus or to possess Him more—by that cast of love which is more desire than repose in possession—you can obtain for mankind, bent towards the earth, that they shall desire, even though confusedly, Him who is all Love.

This is how the Holy Spirit will work in your hearts, and it is well that you should know what direction He will lead you in, so that you may avoid hampering His action and, at the same time, be more at ease in this kind of prayer. Here, as always, Jesus Himself is the model; and His more especial call to

us is to live over the prayer that welled up in Him
when, already tired from journeying on the hot,
dusty roads, He would be so pressed by the crowd of
the poor and the sick, so jostled and harried by them
all with their beseechings, that He would even be
unable to find time to eat—it is this prayer He wishes
us to share with Him, the kind that brought to His
lips those words recorded by St. Mark, "I am moved
with pity for the multitude; it is three days now since
they have been in attendance upon me, and they have
nothing to eat" (Mark 8:2); the kind that made Him
take "pity on them, since they were like sheep that
have no shepherd" (Mark 6:34); the kind that made
Him cry out, ". . . and now my soul is distressed. What
am I to say? I will say, Father, save me from under-
going this hour of trial . . ." (John 12:27).

It will likewise be the oppressed, blood-drawing
prayer at Gethsemani, when Jesus, in agony, offered
Himself to the Father with the piercing vision of
men's misery before His eyes—that misery which you
will elbow every day; which nothing should make you
forget. It will also be the prayer that still kept burn-
ing, like the small, wavering flame of a night-lamp
hidden under the thick, heavy, smothering mantle
of His suffering body, as He dragged Himself over
the stones with the crushing weight of the Cross on
His back, and as He writhed in the last struggle upon
it. Prayer in the peace and repose of contemplation was far away indeed (though it might, of course,
have been otherwise, had it been otherwise willed)
when Jesus came to the great act of His life, to the

act that was to be the great proof of His love, to the act that saved the world.

What good reason could there be *for not consecrating a religious life more especially to allowing Jesus to live such prayer over again in us*? If we were to attempt to introduce into our life as Little Brothers a type of prayer like that of the Carthusian or the solitary, we should quickly become divided against ourselves; we should have wagered against the impossible. We have left behind, once for all, the conditions requisite to solitary contemplation, and this for love of our fellow men; nor has Jesus ever demanded that all who wish to follow Him should employ that form of prayer. What He has insistently urged, on the other hand, is perseverance up to continual prayer. The action of the Holy Spirit is quite many-sided enough to be able to give birth to, and then establish, in us a way of praying which will be both continual and pressing—the kind, I mean, that Jesus bids one to when He says one must pray "at all times," which is also the kind we promised to assume to the full extent of our generosity when we became Little Brothers. The Little Brothers' prayer, in other words, is to be no different in nature from that which Jesus asks of *all men*, all sinners; and we must seek to make ourselves perfect in it.

It is not Jesus' custom to mock the poor and the humble; anything He requires of us is always *possible* with His help. To help carry to the perfection of love the prayer of the publican, of the woman taken in adultery, of all the sick and the maimed and the blind that besieged Jesus day and night—such is the grace we must open our hearts to. Then our prayer will come straight from our lives and not from outside them. It is there, too, that it will find its nourishment, because we shall have learned to see all things *in faith*, with the eyes of the Lord Himself.

But while our participation in the toil and suffering of the world is our starting-point for a life entirely offered up in prayer, we should never be unmindful of the fact that our prayer must likewise be *adoration*, and adoration on behalf of the many. Our continual contact with people might well tend to make us forgetful of this. Regular exposition of the Blessed Sacrament, bringing one back as it does into the presence of Jesus sacrificed to the Father for all mankind; our night adoration, our days of monthly retreat, and the existence of the Adoration Fraternities will, however, keep us reminded of this other side of our vocation, and therefore of all our prayer must be; otherwise, we should be running the risk of forgetting that it is Jesus' desert to be loved and worshipped for Himself, to have time "wasted" on Him for His own sake, even while there are people weeping and suffering in the world.

This loss-of-time-for-love's-sake guise under which the pure act of prayer will sometimes come to us is also a means of verifying the quality of our faith in the divine transcendence and so purifying our relationships with others. In an atmosphere of materialism, where efficiency is fast becoming an absolute criterion of a man's worth, people will seldom understand this side of our lives, that seemingly "serves no good purpose" and "does nobody any good." There is a hidden source of temptation for us here, a temptation which, in the end, might lead to the weakening of our faith in the mystery of God without our realizing it sufficiently.

Some of you may wonder whether our night adoration or our solitary retreats may not prove conducive to prayer like that of the cloistered religious. My answer would be this. Jesus is, of course, free to do as He likes, and can therefore pour contemplation into our souls in torrents, if He will. Yet it would hardly seem to me, even in that event, that our way of contemplating the mystery of God could ever be quite the same as that of the solitary contemplative. Our minds would very likely be too unaccustomed to abandoning themselves to that form of prayer, and our bodies too heavy with fatigue. The important thing for us is to let the Spirit of Jesus have His way, with all the generosity in us. It is Jesus' own silent adoration of the Father that must come into us through the Holy Eucharist. And since we shall not be able to leave behind the weight of other souls with their misery, our prayer will be more like what occurred with Jesus when, worn with fatigue, He would go up into a mountain to pray in secret, carrying with Him (how, indeed, could the Redeemer have done otherwise?) the whole load of the moral and physical sufferings He had seen displayed before Him in the course of the day.

Perhaps we shall thus reach a purer kind of adoration. Adoration is admiration of the supreme mystery of the Divinity, hidden in eternity. Jesus has shown us that that mystery is all one of love and mercy, for it was expressed in its entirety in the divine acts of the incarnation and the redemption. Adoration that comes from a heart completely open to its neighbor is therefore the truest and purest kind of adoration. It is none too easy to say exactly what I mean here and I must leave it to you to grasp it. But you may be sure that it all consists, whatever your prayer may be like at any time, in connecting it up with the Heart of Jesus and, when you have done all you can yourselves, opening up your emptiness to Him and letting Him fill it with His own prayer. The trouble, of course, is that we are so loath to admit our emptiness. We always want to have *something that is ours* to give. But perfection, even where prayer is concerned, lies in being able to accept one's indigence.

II

The Religious Life
of the
Little Brothers of Jesus

". . . contemplatives thrust straight
into the world and the world's
misery."

—Jacques and Raissa Maritain,
Liturgy and Contemplation

4

THE MEANING
OF THE NAME

If Father de Foucauld chose the name "Little Brothers of Jesus" for his disciples to come, it was not just because he was fond of it as a term, but because it seemed to him so aptly to express the ideal that had formed itself in his mind and heart. Since that ideal is our vocation, I want here to help you to realize the full meaning of our name and, at the same time, to see to what it binds us.

I

Brothers to Jesus is literally what we are to be with our entire lives. We are not giving ourselves only to an ideal, however great; we are not giving ourselves only to the pursuit of a perfection, however true; we are giving ourselves to a Person, a living person who is God, and a God who is our brother in the most absolute sense of the word, because He is also a man. Of all the reasons for the life we have chosen, the Christ-Jesus is the sum and substance.

First and last, our effort of faith will be in the direction of a most personal meeting, certain as we are that we cannot lose our way if we adhere to our Lord with our beings, if we place our lives and our very selves in His hands—in the hands of Him who is the Way itself, Truth itself, Life itself. Everything in us must therefore tend to simplify itself in a union with Him in those places where we shall find Him alive, namely in our faith, in the Eucharist, in the Gospel, and in our brother men. If we wish to make the gift of ourselves to our brother men, it is again, on account of Him.

In a world as unsettled as is ours today, a world in the midst of whose confusion man has to think out a city of the future which shall be fraternal, just and favorable to the human person, nothing is easy, everything is complicated. The number of problems which are posed simultaneously, and on a scale now enlarged to the dimensions of the universe, is so great, and they bring into play such a tangled mass of values of all descriptions on all the different planes of social and economic life, that the human mind, with its natural limitations and its inherent weaknesses, is as if overawed. Faced with the immensity of the effort entailed and the complexity of the techniques required, people's minds are apt to become absorbed to a point where they will entirely lose sight of the one thing which lends meaning to the world, the existence of Jesus, their Christ. Even for the most sincere Christian, involved in the gigantic task by love—for surely it is one of the obligations of Christian love to work for the cessation of injustice on the earth and the establishment of conditions for all which shall be not only human but Christian—even for the most sincere Christian, I say—yes, even for the apostle—there is a great temptation in thinking that one does not have the time to look towards Jesus and love Him as He should be loved: for Himself.

Our role, Little Brothers, our particular task is right here: to act as the "regard" of men of today upon Jesus, to be the "standing delegates" in Jesus' presence of the forgetful crowd, carrying to Him in their place their adoration, their needs, their complaints and their faults. A Little Brother *must* be close to Jesus, wherever he is. There is therefore but one direction to which he *may* turn—and turn continually and indefatigably—in his gropings towards love, and that is to Jesus Himself, because the source of his life *is* Jesus.

We can learn from Father de Foucauld how thus to go straight to Jesus and live for Him, simply and naturally, once we have seen Him as He really is in the Gospel.

Father de Foucauld leads us back to essentials and teaches us to simplify our lives. For, if he points a way that is simplicity itself, he makes no attempt either to soften or to evade, with the help of any would-be new method or recipe, those of the Gospel exigencies which are sometimes blunt and brutal. The

view he holds is that the expedient thing for love, in
its eagerness, is to take the path that goes right up
and leads straight to the goal with no detours or
meanders. In this he was a faithful disciple of Fran-
cis of Assisi, of John of the Cross, and of Therese of
Lisieux. How many ways do you think there are of
loving? How many ways are there of giving oneself?
There is only one: the strong way, the complete way,
the heroic way. Of those who really mean to serve
Him, Jesus requires nothing less.

II

This name of ours also expresses better than any
other name could do, the manner in which we are
to love one another, and love all other men as well.
If we are to be of any "use" at all in the world, it will
be for having been faithful enough to allow a bit of
Christ's immense love for men to appear through *our*
hearts and *our* comportment. But to have been given
a mission to make Jesus' Gospel, His beatitudes and
His loving friendship for the poor "present" by living
in the world, is something much too big for us to be
able to discover entirely in a single stroke.

Moreover, the world has little need for us to present it with any mere "new formula" or "state" of the
religious life; people are dying of hunger and thirst
because they are so far away from Him who is Life,
and what they want is a presence: the presence of
Life; unknowingly, they are seeking a person—a divine person—and this person is Love Incarnate, Jesus.

Even the perfect achievement of an "ideal to live by" would not be enough for them. This is something much more exacting, much more difficult; but it is our vocation as Little Brothers.

Abstract phrases, however well thought-out, however all-embracing, however complete they may seem to us; terms like "silence," "hidden-life," "mixing with the environment," "mere presence," "witness," "non-efficacy," etc., may all help to characterize our outer existence, but none of them, either singly or all together, can define it. So let us have no other point of reference than Jesus at Nazareth, with the will to imitate Him with all our love. If we are really united with our Lord, if we keep our eyes trained upon Jesus living and working at Nazareth, then, like Father de Foucauld, we shall be able to remain open to people's solicitations and meet them as our mission in the Church requires.

We too must therefore dare, like Brother Charles, to break through phrases and formulas that are too rigid, definitions that are too narrow, so long as we remain faithful to this same close imitation and this same intimate union with our Lord. We too hunger for our Lord, hunger to follow Him in His real and sincerely desired poverty; hunger to see achieved in us all that He proclaimed blessed on the mount in Galilee; hunger to give Him our love, to look upon Him, to contemplate Him in continual prayer; hunger to enter into His redeeming love, and therefore to love our fellow men as He did, and especially the poorest among them; to love them out of live friendship, for themselves, each as if he were the only soul to be loved in the world, without seeking "results" or apostolic "output" at all costs and, likewise, without measuring our efforts as if with a foot ruler or forever comparing them with some abstract definition of what our life should be.

It is, indeed, impossible to love Jesus and love men with and through Him without being possessed by a desire to give Him to the world, and so meet the call of so many souls that are hungering for God's real kingdom. How could we help wanting to give out something of the light and strength and peace and joy which we have in our souls because we belong to Jesus? "Nobody lights a lamp, to hide it away in a jar or under a bed; it is put on a lamp-stand, so that all who come into the house can see its light" (Luke 8:16).

The lamp in us has been put there by Jesus, and has been lit by Him in the measure in which we have given ourselves to Him. It is not therefore for us but for Him to say whether it is to be put on a lamp-stand so that its light may be seen. But since He has lit it, why should He not wish it to light and illumine and warm men's hearts? Yet it is not for us to place it on a lamp-stand, either. We must let Him do as He likes, because we belong to Him. Nor need we be concerned for fear our lamp may not burn; if it has really been lit by Jesus, if it has really been put on the lamp-stand by Jesus, the wind that blows in through the door opening to the wayfarer will not put it out. Jesus wishes us to be the "light of the world," the "salt of the earth," and the "leaven in the bread." This is a matter of "being," not of "doing." All our desire, all our work must be to be so united with Jesus that we shall *become* light, become salt, become leaven *with Him*. The rest is not our business. But Jesus also wishes us *present* in the world's midst. We must therefore be ready to be devoured by those who hunger and thirst for God's holiness.

We may not be recognized for what we are; we may be misunderstood, despised, rejected. Blessed shall we be, then—provided it be for the sake of Christ. But if it be for not having let His message pass through with enough purity, let us beware! There is always a certain tendency for us to tarnish or diminish the message with our personal limitations; and its power is then lost. If we are despised or rejected for Jesus' name, we must, of course, be glad, but our hearts must be torn at the same time, for this will mean that people are still unable to detect the Savior's passing, or else that it is a scandal to them. Yet, *at the same time*, the fact remains that Jesus Himself was despised and rejected, and may therefore call upon us to share that mystery of abjection and agony with Him.

If those among whom we live come with eagerness to light themselves by our lamp and drink from our spring of living water, we must first take care to be littler, poorer, more abandoned to Jesus, and then let them warm themselves, let them drink, and allow ourselves to be devoured by these men who are so much poorer than we because they have not yet found the

Kingdom. So long as our love has not reached the point where it has made us truly capable of showing them that the Kingdom of Jesus is for them, and that it has even begun to be present in their midst through us, we shall not have met the demands of Jesus' love upon us. The Kingdom must be able to appear to them through us in all its realness: the patience, the peace, the force of Christ, and also Christ's demands for justice—all this enveloped, as it were, in love and void of all hatred (even when it is right to fight). Of the truth of the Kingdom we must deliver all. In certain environments, it will take a tremendous effort to avoid violating any side of it.

What Jesus requires of us above all else is that we give ourselves in utterly disinterested friendship; that we love fraternally and tenderly all those He sends us and especially the most forsaken and those who suffer most. With our modern civilization, based so much on the technical, there is a stronger and stronger trend— due precisely to our constantly increasing technical proficiency—towards "rationalization" in the satisfaction of men's needs, these being scientifically classified, labelled and divided up among as many official Services or Departments. If this tendency continues to excess—and this is already the case in certain spheres in various countries—a man will be treated less and less like a person—I mean, like the unique being each one is, with a heart of his own, sufferings of his own, his own problems, his own joys and a family which belongs to nobody but him. He will be a being without a name, and all that will be seen in him by these Services will be his diseases—to be cured for him; his lack of money—to be met for him; his want of a roof—to be provided for him; and his need of free time and leisure—to be organized for him. The more exaggeration there is with the will to cure and improve and facilitate, the more technique will have to be resorted to—indeed, in the very name of ordinary fraternal love and likewise where fraternal love has its source in God and is therefore "charity"—and this will involve more and more unwieldy administrative machinery where men's hearts will no longer be recognized for what they are.

Obviously, nobody can deny the necessity of technique and technology, but man nevertheless easily becomes a slave to it all, and it would seem that Christian laymen and Christian priests and religious must submit to their laws, at the risk of being enslaved themselves, in order to put them at the service of love.

It does not, of course, come within our vocation to organize works of either bodily or spiritual welfare, with or without a view to maximum efficiency. That is not what Jesus asks of us. What, on the other hand, He does want is this: as a supreme testimony, as a sort of counterweight to the world rush to technology, to which the Church's apostolate in the world risks succumbing, that we should love a handful of men who are miserable, poor, sick—those He will choose for us—and that we should love them, as I have said, with friendship, tenderly, like persons and not like cases for assistance. It will moreover often be beyond our ability to mitigate their sufferings, much as we must always try to do so with the feeble means at our disposal.

Jesus wishes us to be dedicated to the love of our brother men, but our refusal to sacrifice the fraternal character of our love to results or efficiency must not make people think that we condemn the proper Christian use of the most highly developed techniques. Our refusal—or rather the attitude from which it results— occurring as it does on the plane of charity, must be a witness of the manner in which Jesus unceasingly loves each one of *His* brothers, and will in fact be a participation of that love in act.

III

Now, another point. Never forget that we are *little*.

Little we are before the task we have to accomplish, as I have now tried to make you see it in the light of Love's demands. Yet, rather than overwhelming us, the disproportion should throw us inwardly upon the force of Jesus. Our radical incapacity must be transmuted into the self-abandonment of the child, with the certainty of being heard by dint of prayer, desire, perseverance and humility. ". . . unless you go back, and become like little children, you shall not enter the kingdom of heaven" (Matt. 18:3). "Such a thing is impossible to man's powers, but to God all things are possible" (Matt. 19:26).

Little we shall also be in the eyes of men. All our lives we shall remain "unprofitable servants," and we must wish, too, so to be dealt with. There will be no task of the apostolate or ministry normally definable as such, as you already know, and there will therefore be no computable output to enhance our life or give it meaning in many people's eyes. We shall be known for religious consecrated to Jesus, but we shall often not even have the appearance of it; and, in any event, we wish no honor or consideration for it. Belonging to the class of the poor as we do, we must accept their sufferings and their servitudes with them, and do everything we can faithfully to keep "the last place."

Jesus wants us to be poor and little, really poor and really little. We are not only to have the spirit of poverty, or the virtue of poverty, which is compatible with any kind of activity or undertaking; we are to *be* poor among the poor, workers among the workers, "little people" among the little people in the world; and this is a choice which involves fearful demands. Jesus wishes us both to belong to the class of the poor and to be considered and treated as such. No vocation could be more positive; and is it not likewise a true apostolic mission to be called to live in poverty amid the miseries of a world where the Church of the poor and poor religious—the countenance of Christ's poor—would be so welcome to so many?

Once you have thoroughly grasped your mission as an overflowing of Jesus' love aiming, through you, to reach with the call of the Beatitudes men who no longer believe in them or have never known what they were, you will at the same time have come to realize that no activity which would take you out of that state and deprive you of being "known as of the poor" could be in keeping with Jesus' will for you; it would, on the contrary, be a misapplication of your charity and your zeal.

But, oh, how pure our poverty must be! How closely it must resemble Jesus's own poverty and not alone that of our fellow men! Jesus wishes to live over again in us the poverty He knew at Nazareth, and this is why we must be poor. We shall have the strength—the strength and the light—to let Him do so, if we keep our eyes fixed upon Him. "Lord Jesus, how quickly will he be poor, he who, loving You with all his heart, cannot abide being richer than his beloved Master! . . ." [1]

It is no narrow conception of poverty or poverty of one single sort I am speaking of, but poverty which is life, and thus capable of being the image of God's own poverty. Jesus' poverty can no doubt find expression in His Little Brothers with very different modalities, according to the environments they are in and also according to the particular cast of each one's personal vocation. But there must be no restricting of the liberty of the Holy Spirit or of the wealth of the life of Jesus among us, and no single brother could render all the different aspects of Jesus' poverty in him, for

---

[1] J. de Gigord, *Ecrits Spirituels de Charles de Foucauld*, Paris, p. 105.

Jesus' poverty is not a lack; neither is it something negative: it is fullness of life in all its simplicity.

IV

But none of this can be real and genuine unless our hearts are changed and become humble, freed of self-love, surrendered beyond question to the love of Jesus crucified. That is the work of a lifetime, a work to be begun again each morning.

You will only succeed in being poor in the way Jesus wishes, you will only have the courage to take upon yourselves the suffering of the workers and the sick, you will only be able to love with hearts humble and fraternal enough, if you are united with Jesus. To envisage prayer and union with Jesus simply as a means for attaining the life of the Gospel would be a temptation which I should not like to see you have. It would amount to turning things upside-down and failing completely to understand Father de Foucauld. But what words of mine can make you realize that Jesus *is* the *whole* of your lives; that He must be your *one* love, your other loves being but its overflowing; and that it is likewise Jesus Himself that both the world and each person in it are living in hopes of?

This is the kind of testimony which the world of today awaits. Man's relations with God have perhaps been made too complicated. People reason too much. There is also too much insistence on means and methods and techniques—yes, even in the spiritual life and the apostolate. Let your intimacy with Jesus be sim-

ple and natural; let it be simply and naturally ardent—*your* force and *your* light.

Like Father de Foucauld, we must have *faith* in Jesus, "Master of the Impossible." We know we have
been called by Jesus, and so we must *believe* it and
draw from this belief the courage to follow through
with a vocation which may require us to dare for Jesus' sake things we would at present look upon as
akin to heroism.

It was faith like this that led Father de Foucauld
constantly to the Eucharist; it is likewise through
faith like this, as also in the Eucharistic Sacrifice, that
we must achieve the same tender and virile friendship with the person of Jesus. At no time was Jesus
ever someone far away, or merely an abstract idea to
Father de Foucauld. That would have been impossible for him to imagine, even when he was fighting in
the darkness of faith to keep a personal, but for the
time being unfelt, contact with Him or to continue
to pray with patient perseverance when it took courage and was sometimes painful for him to do so. In
this Father de Foucauld must be our model. A passive
attitude, where the Holy Spirit would be expected to
do all the work, was as foreign to his mind as the
over use of any method for directing one's thoughts
towards God would have been. What strikes one
about his way of praying, on the contrary, is that he
simply took himself and put himself into it manfully,
unreservedly, fervently, with his whole will and the
whole of his being.

Little Brothers, we must learn to remain united with Jesus in each and every situation, however difficult this may appear at times. Nor must we wait for it to happen by itself, free gift from God as it all is. Once we have "cast into God" our maddest hopes and our utmost confidence, it is up to us to put the best in us—the best in our minds and the best in our hearts—courageously at the service of our prayer and "presence" to Jesus, with the simplest and most unequivocal of methods.

Brother Charles would not only sit at Jesus' feet in the Eucharist and keep his eyes fixed upon Him in silence; he also always meditated on His words in the Gospel, so as to keep his life in tune with them. If we too read the Gospel with the same eyes of love and succeed in receiving the words of Jesus in our hearts like imperative commands to be translated into acts, the Gospel will become a living rule of life for us. The better we follow it, the better we shall comprehend it. Any light that may come to us, however feeble, we must never fail to put immediately into our lives. Nothing is more vain or more wearing than meditating on a truth or a moral value and merely keeping it in the mind—meditating "in circles," in other words—without putting it into practice. "I cannot conceive of love that feels no constraining need of resembling and becoming like You."

It was by successive stages, and not all at once, that Father de Foucauld came into complete possession of his vocation. In other words, his spiritual life started with a germ and grew little by little to maturity, all quite naturally. So will it be with each Little Brother. However deep his desire, however great his generosity, it will take time for him to become capable of bearing witness to Jesus and His Gospel in a life of prayer lived in the midst of mankind. He must grow to it and, in order to grow to it, he will have to pass through successive phases the duration, and even the order, of which will be different in each individual case. But a phase of "hidden life" and solitude, a phase of active toil and of experience in making the gift of self in the world, and a phase of study and reflection are necessary for all. I do not, however, consider that these different phases of training will invariably necessitate the Brothers' living under definitely corresponding external circumstances; I believe it may sometimes be more a matter of their holding to different inner attitudes individually, whatever the circumstances, as they follow what the Holy Spirit asks of them.

To find Jesus, to love Jesus, to live for Jesus; to be literally and unremittingly possessed by a great desire to love each and every man with the true devotion of a brother; to be eager to be little on earth— that, Little Brothers of Jesus, is what your name means. That, too, is what you must strive to bring about in your lives by handing them over, in humble, confident self-abandonment, to the action of the Spirit of Love.

CHAPTER

5

"SAVIORS WITH JESUS"

When people inquire about our Fraternities I always find it awkward to answer clearly once they get on to the "What-kind-of-a-life-is-it?" and "What-are-your-activities?" and "What-sort-of-a-schedule-do-you-follow?" plane with their queries. This is all beside the question. I feel quite incapable of expressing the whole of our ideal in any formula; quite apart from the fact that, at first sight, our life appears in certain respects to be complex and inconsistent. For the Little Brother must be at one and the same time a worker and a man of prayer—a man of silence, who must also be alive and attentive to the cares and concerns of his brothers and his friends; a completely detached contemplative, but with a certain freedom of movement and a certain freedom in the use of things. These apparent contradictions must resolve themselves in the simplicity of the inner principle of our life. This, then, is the thing to be defined; the rest is only part of its consequences.

"I cannot conceive of love that feels no constraining need of resembling, of becoming like You, and especially sharing all the hurts and pains, all the difficulties, all the hardships of life. . . . I judge no one,
Lord; the others are also your servants, and my brothers, and I must just love them. . . . But it is impossible for me myself to understand how one can love
You and not seek to resemble You, and not feel the
need of sharing every cross." The call we have heard
is this same call; and so it is that we have been led to
choose Father de Foucauld as our guide. Loving our
Lord, we wish to share His labor and His sufferings.
Loving men, our brothers, we wish to share the life
of the poor, of those who suffer, simply out of love.
That is why we find, in actually carrying out our
ideal, that we have equal need for prayer and detachment and for working with men in their weariness and their poverty.

We encounter difficulties, risks and conflicts in the
undertaking. It could not be otherwise. So it behooves
us to have a firm grasp upon the initial attitude which
must constantly underlie this kind of life. This attitude can be summed up by saying that, out of love for
Christ, we must desire to share Christ's suffering. To
be more precise, I mean the suffering of Christ *the
Savior*; for all our suffering, and even that which
comes from sharing other people's afflictions, thus becomes a continuation in us of Jesus' Passion. This
orientation is something fundamental and, unless we
possess it, I do not believe any one of us can either
really understand the meaning of our life as Little
Brothers or bear the weight of it.

"Jesus" means "God who saves," and the name is so dear to us—as it was to Father de Foucauld—for this reason. It expresses the whole of the reason for Christ's existence. He was indeed all "savior," nothing but "savior," through the Cross. We also have no other reason for our life as Little Brothers. But it is not written in the nature of our beings that we are to be saviors as it was with Jesus. This, moreover, is why it is so hard for us. Yet this vocation for sharing the redemptive suffering is something so essential that, if we were to recoil from giving ourselves up to it completely, our life would cease to be truthful.

So we must entertain no illusions as to what God will ask of us all through our lives. To this end, we can do no better than listen more attentively than we are ordinarily inclined to do to what Jesus replies to those who say that they wish sincerely to follow Him: "You do not know what it is you ask. Have you strength to drink of the cup I am to drink of, to be baptized with the baptism I am to be baptized with? They said to him, We have. And Jesus told them, You shall indeed drink of the cup I am to drink of . . ." (Mark 10:38). It is really their share in the sufferings with which He was to save the world, that Jesus promises His friends, and therefore His Little Brothers. Hence the thing for us to do is to grasp what Jesus demands here with all our faith and as concretely as we can, and then, fully aware of what we are doing, answer with unreserved, whole-hearted, resolute and confident assent.

Obviously, you are not expected to start out fully prepared and knowing to perfection how to take suf-

fering. No one can know this until he has been taught
by our Lord Himself, sometimes through the experience of an entire lifetime. Nor are you expected to
say whether you are certain of being capable of it.
We must simply have clearly understood the meaning
of the Cross in our life, and have generously and
gladly consented to let Jesus take us into His work
with Him. We must be ready, in our souls, to accept
suffering and to learn to comprehend its significance
and to come little by little to love it.

The first temptation to come may be discouragement. Our daily experience has already shown us how
weak we are before the slightest suffering. We are
downcast over the slightest failure, held back by the
slightest fatigue, sickened of praying by the slightest
inner obstacle, wounded by the slightest lack of consideration. We likewise realize that these insufficiencies recur every day, and we ask ourselves how we
can ever really succeed in sharing Jesus' Cross.

Considered from this angle, our problem would
seem to be insoluble, and it is; and you must be thoroughly convinced that it is. Both the painful experience of your personal weakness and the things that
happen to you every day will, moreover, see to it that
this conviction is properly instilled into you. But if
you *want* to love, you can come to desire with all your
hearts that Jesus, through His love, shall make you
capable of sharing His redemptive suffering. A true
desire and a deep desire must come first; then you
must tell Jesus so indefatigably, with the boldness of
the sons of Zebedee and St. Peter. Then you must be

humble enough, simple enough to abandon yourselves to Jesus with utter confidence and assurance
that, by keeping yourselves united with Him, you will
become capable, first, of enduring, and then of loving,
the Cross. Lastly, you must go to work with all your
will and cooperate with God in His action in your
lives.

In all this—as always in the spiritual life—you must
be simple, true, and straightforward. Place yourselves well under the light of honest truth. The object
is not to picture yourselves as any braver or stronger
than you are in face of physical or moral suffering.
Neither is it to make yourselves think you desire
heavier crosses or more difficult tests than you are
actually capable of bearing. No more is it to imagine
yourselves incapable of a braver effort than any you
have so far made. It is mostly a matter of *willing* to
start and making a very definite and joyful effort in
any way accessible to you.

I say you must make a joyful effort. There are two
reasons for this. First, God does not like one to give
forlornly. You must give out of love for Jesus; and
where there is real love of Jesus, there must be joy.
Secondly, you must guard against taking your little
difficulties and daily sufferings too seriously. I keep
harping on these, because they are the very fabric of
our lives. If we can succeed in turning into live crosses
these things of every day which, though small in
themselves, can become so heavy through constant
repetition, we shall know how to embrace the bigger
ones. Furthermore, we may sometimes be kept wait-

ing a long while for the bigger crosses. Our courage
might then turn out to be more imaginary than real,
and our love, of a quality little different.

In order to avoid self-indulgent reversions, your
offering in immolation should be made with your eyes
fixed on Jesus' Cross and not your own. By getting
away from yourselves, you will lighten your own sufferings (partly by forgetting them) and you can then
really offer them up with greater freedom. For, you
must always remember, it is not the suffering or the
trouble itself that has the redemptive virtue, but the
attitude of oblation in it, the love it arouses and the
degree to which it is united with the Passion of
Christ. The natural flow of our life as Little Brothers
is for our inclusion, with all our personal sufferings, in
the great current of Jesus' Passion and the passion of
the world. This is the direction for us to look in.

"The Passion of Jesus," "the Cross of Jesus"—these
are no doubt words which have lost much of their
meaning, words which have become worn with use.
We must rediscover the reality behind them in all its
concreteness. Penetrating behind the sober wording
of the Gospel, we must become alive to the horrible,
brutally mathematical sufferings which Jesus endured
to the ultimate depths of both body and soul. Against
the humiliations, the insults, the contempt, the mon-
strous physical and mental pain, and the anguish and
the agony suffered by Him whom we claim to love—
the Son of God!—we must place our all too miserable
little trials and difficulties. Between the Cross on
which Jesus hung bleeding and our day of today, our

lives at this moment, there is a living bond, an actual connection; and it is this that we must become more especially conscious of. Upon each moment in our days, there is some of Jesus' blood. It is there as an unassailable proof of love and a pledge of strength.

Then there is the mystery of all the suffering in the world, all the distress of mankind, which you will find more and more disconcerting. It must be viewed in the perspective of the Cross. But, first of all, be well aware of its existence; do not let yourselves turn aside. Be aware of it tangibly, concretely. You have plenty of opportunity to do so; it is all around you. Of this whole great passion of the world you must grasp the mystery and the meaning.

What weight can your days have against it? you may ask. Your personal suffering, you may be certain, amounts indeed to very little; it nevertheless becomes all-powerful if it serves as a bond between the Cross of Christ and this great—and often just formless and featureless—mass of human affliction. Insofar as the spirit of self-immolation in you is pure and full of courage and love, it causes a bit of the divine life to penetrate into this immense distress, plants the Cross of Jesus there; and thus, through you, with your help, it acquires a meaning: it becomes more a part of Jesus' Passion continuing in His Mystical Body.

So, do not cut yourselves off from what brings suffering to others, but never let yourselves be crushed by suffering. Be particularly careful to avoid the delusion that it is enough if you sympathize with your feelings. True communion in the suffering of Christ, and in that of our fellow men, is of another sort. Contradictory as this may seem, it should not breed depression or sadness but, on the contrary, the strength and peace which union with Christ always brings when it is real. No, no excessive emotion before suffering, whether it be yours or someone else's; no mere sensitivity, above all; that sort of feeling simply empties the soul of its strength, and prevents the real kind of love.

Nor must you yield to bitterness before the unbearable sight of other people's suffering, or its seeming unfairness, or when you see them rebel against it. Keep your souls in peace and gentleness. More especially still, do not allow your own sufferings, whatever their cause and however unwarranted you may think them, to arouse bitterness or resentment in you. You must be absolutely frank and loyal with yourselves on this point, and keep a perfectly open mind. Bitterness almost always comes from wounded self-esteem or from pride insufficiently subdued. Let us not be too quick either to lay responsibility for this kind of feeling at other people's doors or to accuse circumstances. Peace, together with the gentleness we must also have with ourselves, returns with humility and the spirit of childhood.

The true spirit of self-immolation presupposes that we behave towards suffering—again, both our own and that of others—as Jesus Himself behaved towards suffering. What is expected of us here is a *compassion*, a communion in the work of redemption, which is understandable only within the plans of

God; and Christ alone—Christ as both God and man—
can show us how to comprehend it and how to carry
it as we must.

Only insofar as we allow Christ crucified really to
live His own sentiments over again in us shall we be
"saviors with Him." Such is the whole mystery of the
Sacred Heart. To grasp the role which suffering plays
in redemption, one must have an infinite sense of the
mercy of God the Father, of His holiness and His justice, coupled with knowledge of the heart of man,
and of his misery, and a strong and tender love for
men. This can be found altogether only in the mind
and heart of the Son of Man. We can obtain it,
through prayer, if we desire it ardently enough, ask
for it often enough, and make ourselves little enough
to receive it. By displaying courage in bearing our
trials and sharing those of others, we shall be beginning our apprenticeship for what God will little by
little put in our hearts. Our prayer and our daily actions will thus come to meet in a single reality: our
life with Jesus—Jesus crucified, Jesus suffering in His
Mystical Body. Without such prayer, the spirit of
self-immolation cannot descend into us, and we
should merely be aping it out of presumption. Without the testing of our courage, our prayer would be
liable to become illusory. It requires all this together
to be able to participate in Jesus' work of redemption
on the Cross.

I hope I have now made clear how absolutely fundamental it is for you to achieve this disposition to

live in a *state* of self-immolation, and also how important it is that this disposition be healthy, truthful and sincere, and well-rooted in faith in Christ. Actually, it is subjacent to your prayer, to your work, and to the thousand and one things that happen to or around you every day. Turning all to use, it can transfigure all and cause all to fructify for the good of those we are called to love. Nothing in our days is then useless, nothing is without its meaning, and there are no more failures; or rather, failures, when they come, bear fruit. Remember that, from the human point of view, Christ's passion was a failure; so too were the life of Charles de Foucauld and the kind of death he met at Tamanrasset. Our own failures and limitations need not be excluded from a like transfiguration by love, provided they finish off in a hymn of humility and self-abandonment. It will take many a day to establish ourselves in this state of immolation, but the important thing is to begin working towards it at once.

Offering oneself thus to suffering out of love, which, as I have suggested, becomes little by little an habitual disposition when one combines one's efforts with the action of the Holy Spirit, is but a development of the quality of a victim stamped upon one's soul with baptism. We all know that one exercises this quality liturgically if one offers oneself really with Christ at the Mass. There is therefore no need for me to emphasize here the primary importance of the Eucharistic Sacrifice in our life as "saviors with Jesus."

The Mass does, however, enable us to accede to the maximum of this communion with Christ crucified and offering Himself, this communion of which our own life of self-immolation must become a day-long continuation. It is the Eucharistic Sacrifice itself—now no longer something exterior to us, for we are then actually integrated into it—that thus fructifies through us.

Living thus in the spirit of sacrifice for others, we shall also be making effective in our lives the mysterious bonds by which we are united to other men in the Mystical Body. The solidarity on the human plane which is affirming itself more and more today in the world of the workers, as also in connection with the organization of society, has a hidden but infinitely more real and more fertile side to it: the solidarity of all men in Christ; and this we must really live. By putting ourselves in the midst of people with this spirit of complete spiritual solidarity and self-immolation and reparation, we shall therefore be giving our life as Little Brothers not only its proper outward appearance, but also its true meaning. Workers with the workers, Arabs with the Arabs, Colored with the Colored, Easterners with the Easterners, Westerners with the Westerners—this we are, or shall be, by a profound gift of self; and our "belonging" will express itself through our unreserved desire for the same destiny and the common suffering. So you can easily see how incomplete, how purely exterior our gift would remain in the end, unless it were carried to the point of spiritual substitution before God. *You must, then,*

*actually succeed in offering yourselves for a ransom
for your brother men.* There will be no imagination
or vain desire about this. In the measure of your communion in the Passion, you will find a great reality
embracing your entire lives—provided only that you
have truly delivered yourselves up to Christ crucified,
with no thought for yourselves.

May what I have now said help you to see better
how you will be giving unity to your lives by establishing your souls in this state of self-immolation, how
your lives will become one long single action turned
in the direction of God, a single every-moment oblation. This is what makes the life of the Little Brother
a true contemplative life, though a contemplative life
with its own "coloring" to it, due to this particular
spirit of reparation and redemption.

CHAPTER

6

"STANDING DELEGATES
TO PRAYER"

The life we have chosen, at the call of Christ, like Brother Charles, is a life which means being totally "present" both to God—with prayer which shall be prayer of adoration and of reparation for the world—and to men—in a poverty and a charity which shall be real and sincere poverty and real and sincere charity. To achieve this ideal is nothing easy, and there must be no delusions in your minds in this respect; it will require an effort of faith and of self-detachment constantly renewed and relentlessly pursued all through your lives.

Every man is naturally "present" to the reality of this visible world in which he has his being and to which he adheres with all his senses. The Christian, and, in a special way, the contemplative, must also be "present" to invisible reality. The thing which marks a man of prayer is precisely this awareness, this re-

sponsiveness, this active aliveness to the entire universe or, in other words, to the world of visible things,
which he touches with his senses, and that of invisible
things, which he reaches through faith, at one and the
same time. He must be the more present to things invisible as they are the more real, in the full sense of
the word "real." The Carthusian monk or the Carmelite nun leaves the visible world in order to reach the
better the reality of the invisible world. The vocation
of the Little Brothers is to embrace both simultaneously.

This duality in his life and perspective divides a
man of faith and makes him, in a way, a stranger
among those of his fellow men who do not possess
this vision of another world. You have no doubt already experienced this feeling and you may be certain that it will return with acuteness. Whether with
people of your own kind or people of other countries
and races or with your working mates or mere
passers-by, you will feel at once very close to them
and very far away; and, at times, this feeling will be
so strong as to be painful. You will feel something like
isolation, coupled with a sense of powerlessness at
your inability to communicate to those around you
this vision which your love for them nevertheless
makes you long to obtain for them. Try as you may,
you will never succeed in being completely one of
them; there will always be this inner attentiveness to
another reality, and people will feel it in you and it
will make you seem strange, and even incomprehensi-
ble, to those who do not believe. So it was with Christ

on earth, utterly present as He was to His surroundings and, at the same time, mysteriously absent—with
a feeling of solitude infinitely more profound and
more painful than anything you will ever experience.
Mary received the shock of this distant absentness in
her Son with violence the day He had remained behind in the Temple.

It would be a grave mistake to try and do away
with either this feeling itself or the outward consequences it involves. The day we cease to be a certain
kind of problem to people, that day we can tell ourselves that we have stopped bearing the presence of
the Great Invisible among them; we shall no longer
be witnesses to Life and Light. If, on the other hand,
we have a true fullness of love for our fellow men in
us—for each of our fellow men in particular—there
will be nothing to fear, for they will be all but unable
to prevent themselves loving this mystery that they
feel in us, because they will sense it to be the source
of the love reaching them from us and attracting them
towards us.

How, then, are you to achieve this complete aliveness to the invisible world? It will be the work of
faith in you, faith developing to the point of being
regularly active in your lives and becoming like an inner eye open towards the things of God and ever
ready to receive their inspirations. The source—and
also the expression—of this "regard of faith" lies in
prayer. A Little Brother must be "on standing service"
for prayer. I think this expression fairly aptly de-
scribes what the attitude of your souls both towards

God and towards men should be. It seems to me to suggest quite clearly your particular vocation for prayer with its various characteristics.

A man "on standing service" is one who has made himself, or has been made, *available* for a special task with a view to the good of all concerned. Likewise with the Little Brother, who must be in an inner state of *continual availability for prayer*.

A man "on standing service" must, as the term itself indicates, assume responsibility for *regular* service, this presupposing a definite continuity in his presence in some particular place. Likewise with the Little Brother, who must become *regularly present to God and Christ* by being—or at least tending to be—lastingly established in the state of prayer.

Again, a man "on standing service" is the object of a *delegation of representation*; and of this he must keep himself constantly reminded if he is to carry out his mandate in the requisite spirit of service. This likewise holds for the Little Brother on the plane of the spiritual responsibilities which he assumes by virtue of the unity of the Mystical Body of Christ, these responsibilities making him literally a standing *delegate to prayer* on behalf of his fellow men.

We must first, then, be completely available for prayer. Now, you will be really available for prayer only if you believe in its vital importance. No one can expect, or be expected, to be entirely available for a task that he does not believe in from the bottom of his heart. On the other hand, a man can go on indefinitely observing a Rule and spending long hours at prayer every day with all the faithfulness and all the goodwill in the world, and still not believe in the importance of prayer. So long as you have not got your very lives and your very souls "involved" in prayer, so to speak; so long as prayer is not the act in which the aspirations of your souls towards the Sovereign Love are expressed most completely; so long as you have not realized that prayer is also that activity in which you are expected to exercise to the maximum your role as mediators and victims, and as delegates of your fellow men; so long as you have not learned all this from living it, and living it personally, with a sense of personal responsibility, despite the fatigue of your daily work, despite the solicitations of things and people and all the activity going on in the world, just so long will there be reason for you to question whether you are yet really available for prayer and whether you are not entertaining illusions in the matter.

There are two sides, or rather two modalities, to our prayer-life. First, there are the *moments of pure prayer* where we cease all worldly activity and withdraw into silence. Secondly, there is—or should be— the *permanent state of prayer* which goes on continuously, whatever one may be doing. Let us deal with the first form first, as is natural—and, furthermore, contrary to what many people think, the second is conditional upon it.

While there is most certainly nothing wrong with aiming to make one's life a continuous and lasting prayer—far from it—it is a very grave error to believe

that moments of regular prayer can lose their usefulness. Pure prayer of this kind is, in fact, both the
source of continual, or what has come to be known
as "diffused," prayer and a higher "activity" indispensable to our relationships with God, which no power
in the world could enable us to dispense with; and,
as such, it is quite simply compulsory. With us Little
Brothers, it has the added importance of a peculiar
duty of our own—adoration before the Blessed Sacrament—which we must discharge not only for our own
sakes but on behalf of mankind.

Surely, no one has ever lived in a more permanent
state of prayer and adoration before God than Jesus
Christ—since the very vision of the Father was constantly present in His soul in the midst of all His
activities as a man. He never stopped praying. His
prayer was perpetual, to such a point that moments
of pure prayer could add neither to its depth nor to
its immediacy. Yet we see Him seizing every opportunity to withdraw into the silence and solitude
of pure prayer.[1] These moments of pure prayer He
would take out of the exhausting days during which
He literally belonged to His disciples, to the sick, to
the multitudes that were always looking for Him,
always pressing Him on all sides. The man in Him
needed these spaces of prayer, free of all human
activity.

---

[1] "When he had finished sending them [the multitudes] home,
he went up by himself on to the hill side, to pray there" (Matt.
14:23). "Then, at very early dawn, he left them, and went away
to a lonely place, and began praying there" (Mark 1:35).

There is a law of our nature as creatures here, and the suspension of human activity—which is the natural outer aspect of prayer—is the very factor by which we can best recognize God's absolute sovereignty over His creatures. God has a right to demand of us that we relinquish our transitory human activities, that we belong exclusively to Him, in His presence. This is what worship, or adoration, is. For a soul that has the sense of God, this is the sort of thing which is self-evident, and it is in the measure in which people lose the sense of the divine—and consequently that of their being as creatures—that they lose the sense of prayer as a necessary "total loss" to themselves in front of God. Prayer of adoration—the essence of true prayer—serves no "useful purpose," in the strict sense of the term, and so long as one fails to see this, one can never really know how to pray. We must seek, first and foremost, to make of our prayer a completely gratuitous work of love and adoration.

Despite all you may believe theoretically about prayer of adoration and your relationships with Jesus and God, it is more likely that you have been approaching prayer—though more unconsciously than not—with some tangible motive, say, to rest and refresh yourselves, or to brace your courage, or something on that order. If you get discouraged with praying, it is probably, in the majority of cases, because, despite everything you have been told in the past about its usefulness, you have not succeeded in observing just where that usefulness lies. When, again, sensible consolations have for some time enabled you to come away from prayer with your souls as if expanded in a state of spiritual felicity or with a feeling of enriching illumination as regards the truths of faith or the Gospel, you have no doubt not realized that it was more than anything else for your own sakes that you had been approaching your adoration with such eagerness. Consequently, when prayer of sheer faith suddenly makes its appearance in you in a state of dryness of the senses and emptiness of the mind, you will be bewildered and disconcerted; and a change of surroundings, or a change of atmosphere, or fatigue from your work will have sufficed to make you so. Or, more simply, it will have sufficed that Jesus stops drawing you to Him with the pull of things exterior to Himself. Discouragement and lassitude as regards prayer will ensue, and you will no longer believe sufficiently in its importance to stick to it. You will then have ceased to be "available" for prayer.

It is, then, of the utmost importance that you be convinced that you go to adoration, not to receive, but to give, and, what is more, to give often without either realizing that you are giving or knowing *what* you are giving. You go to adoration to deliver up to God, in the night of faith, your entire being. You must also realize all that these words "deliver up your entire being to God" mean in the way of obscure faith, in the way of suffering at times, in the way of wealth of love always. Adoration is not, to begin with at least, either a matter of feeling or a matter of thinking, but a matter of recognizing God's legitimate hold upon what is deepest in us—upon our very selves; a work that is something bigger and more absolute than you can be conscious of. It is likewise an act which presupposes a great measure of self-abandonment and a great deal of courage in letting Christ carry on in one an activity which will often be immensely painful. This you must keep repeating to yourselves until you have become sufficiently convinced of it to be able to put it into practice.

With experience, you will come to see to what point true prayer presupposes detachment from everything created. From the moment one starts to pray, there must be an actual sort of death to everything that is not God. This is why so many people, including priests and religious, flee true prayer and take refuge in the mere formality of vocal prayers, which enables them to think they are praying, or else in a meditative sort of reflection on some subject having to do say, with morals. Consciously or unconsciously, these often become ways of regular escape when one fails to accomplish the fundamental act of self-giving which is the necessary preliminary to prayer. This most certainly does not mean, however, that either vocal prayer or reflection on the Gospel and the truths of faith can be done away with. I only say that, in certain cases, they can easily serve as an "alibi" for souls reluctant to go the whole way.

Availability for prayer presupposes, then, not only a thorough belief in the importance of prayer, but a whole very real process of inner detachment, which

must be accepted from its very principle as something both root-deep and unbounded—in other words,
measurable only by the immeasurable love which is
asked of us.

First, then, we must *desire* prayer. It is obvious, I
think, that if this complete giving of ourselves to
Christ is really embodied in our moments of adoration, we shall desire these in the measure in which
our love is genuine. Do not let yourselves imagine,
however, that this desire appears all of itself. It is
something which does not come naturally to man in
his ordinary state. Normally speaking, it is an exercise of faith. An act of faith, in the full sense of the
term, is an act of the will making our entire being—
often in spite of its resistance and in complete obscurity—take an attitude corresponding to the reality
of the invisible world; and this is why nothing is
truer than an attitude or an act of the soul com-
manded by the will out of sheer faith. It is a great
mistake to think that an attitude has to be natural
and spontaneous in order to be true. To fulfil our
being as sons of God, we have to force ourselves to
act in conformity with the invisible, and normally
inaccessible, divine realities.

Faith thus strengthened, and faith alone, will make
you desire your moments of prayer. This desire will
take root in you little by little, thus preparing the way
for pure prayer. But, when all is said and done, the
best way of acquiring the desire to encounter Jesus
thus in your adoration, is to go straight to meet Him.
Drop your wishing and theorizing, then, and make

yourselves available—not just inwardly well disposed, but in actual fact ready—for prayer. Always be prepared to take advantage of a free moment to turn to prayer as the most important thing in your days. If you get into the habit of never giving God any more than the time prescribed by the Rule and feel no need of spending a moment in prayer from time to time, simply because you want to, out of love for our Lord, who is there waiting for you, then you are not yet a real Little Brother. If you consider that it is enough just to do your duty by God by carrying out the prescribed schedule of prayer; if you think of a thousand and one different things to do on a free afternoon, save an extra bit of adoration; if, in the course of your goings and comings, or your travels, it never occurs to you to step into a church and say a prayer when you would have plenty of time to do so, all this will go to show that you are not truly available for prayer. A soul really given to prayer can always find odd moments to pray in, and you know very well—perhaps, indeed, from your own experience—that one desires the divine realities only in the measure in which one already possesses them. So the more you pray, the more you will desire prayer.

To fulfil our vocation, it is not enough to devote particular times in the day to prayer; we must constantly endeavor to follow our Lord's precept regarding continual prayer. Too often, there is a veritable fissure between life and prayer. In order to prevent this, it seems to me that there must be a threefold effort: 1) to "acclimate" our prayer to the everyday life of the environment into which it has to be, so to speak, "injected"; 2) to make it a living act of love and self-giving, and 3) to strive to make genuine prayer of all our actions.

Certain psychological conditions, and certain means of exercising one's faith, are necessary to prayer, and this is the more the case the less one's prayer takes place under the action of the Holy Spirit. It is in connection with these that what I have called "acclimatization" to the actual surroundings must be effectuated. Our spiritual life is very often adapted to a framework which is much too intellectual and this, though seldom realized, is one important reason for many cases of lack of balance—especially among priests and religious—and also for many people abandoning prayer altogether. What happens is a sort of intellectualization of people's inner lives, and they therefore become dependent upon the conditions requisite to an intellectual life, to the point of their inner lives being incapable of subsisting without them.

Let me emphasize that there is but one thing which can bring about unity inside us, as also in our lives—and very specially between prayer and action—and that is love. Jesus' command is that we love God and our fellow men up to death to ourselves. That is perfection. Perfection does not come automatically with any particular status in life, contemplative or not. It is not because one spends habitually long hours at prayer, or even because one embraces, say, the Rule of the Carthusian monk or the Carmelite nun, that one will necessarily accomplish a work of perfection. Leading a contemplative life is not necessary to perfection as such, but love *is*, and always is. Even in the act of true contemplative prayer, it is well to remember those strong words of St. Paul's: "I may speak with every tongue that men and angels use; yet, if I lack charity, I am no better than echoing bronze, or the clash of cymbals. I may have powers of prophecy, no secret hidden from me, no knowledge too deep for me; I may have utter faith, so that I can move mountains; yet if I lack charity, I count for nothing" (1 Cor. 13:1-2). It is therefore essential that anyone who, like ourselves, has been called by God to a contemplative life, should take more care than anyone else to see that his prayer be a work of love, and that it be an authentic and living one.

For prayer must be a vital act done with what makes life in us: faith and love. It is also, therefore, an act of self-giving in which real and actual self-detachment is presupposed. It must also be honest and open, else it cannot be the meeting it should be between yourselves as you are, with your human wretchedness, your fatigue, your sins and your temptations, and Christ standing there between you and God.

You will no doubt have noticed that I keep stressing the effort which faith has to make in searching for God (almost always in obscurity and aridity), without referring to the more or less constant action of the gifts of the Holy Spirit. I do this simply because faith, when left to itself, requires this active effort, whereas, with the action of the Holy Spirit, we merely have to submit when He comes and completes by Himself our often so miserably unproductive effort.

When we go, then, to adoration or to our work or to the service of our fellow men, it must all be with the same purity of intention and the same movement of love. There will then be unity in our lives. Also, there will remain in us, deep in the bottom of our souls, a perpetual desire to love and manifest our love; and this we will do, now by praying in silence, now at our work, now in conversation.

This presupposes that we have gained the proper mastery over ourselves and are really capable of shaking off all human desire. Only on this condition can we dominate the whole of our activities—work and prayer—and make of that whole a multiple expression of a single movement of love. Here we run into solid, indeed very solid, difficulties, which are none other than our temperaments, our passions, our habits and our feelings. There is but one remedy at our disposal here: recourse to energetic and balanced self-discipline, or asceticism, which shall be properly adapted to our immediate state. Lack of self-discipline, and consequently of self-mastery, is one of the great reasons why we fail in our attempts to achieve unity between our lives and our prayer.

Outside your moments of pure prayer, you must, as I began by saying, learn to pray permanently. This

statement requires some explanation; people often
have wrong ideas on the subject, and therefore easily
get discouraged, because they are pursuing an inaccessible objective. The aim, then, is to "pray constantly," or "keep the presence of God," or "institute
diffused prayer throughout one's life." Whichever of
these terms one uses, they all designate one and the
same thing, though with varying nuances corresponding to different states of mind and soul.

Immediately one speaks of "prayer" and "presence," an act of faith is always implied in some degree
or other, and not only an act of love. The link between the two is very close, but I do not think one
can say that our actions or our days are prayer from
the simple fact that we perform and live them out
of love. This would be a misuse of language, and
the upshot of that sort of thing is that words no longer
mean what they are supposed to mean. To pray is to
perform an act in which faith, whether adoring or
requesting, and mind always have some share, with
or without the use of words. To pray is, at the least,
to look towards God; to pray is to think of God, to
speak to God, or to entreat God—whether it be with
spoken words or with ideas or mental images or, more
simply, with the infinitely deeper but obscure regard
of contemplation. When there is none of this, one
cannot say that prayer exists, in the proper sense of
the word.

How then are we going to succeed in prolonging
prayer throughout the day? How can we make a continuous prayer out of all our actions? A sacrifice can

be considered to be a prayer in act, in the broad sense of the term. Here, already, our lives can be a prayer in this sense, if they are explicitly offered up, more especially in union with the Eucharistic Sacrifice. A disposition like this, when explicitly renewed at each Mass, really does give all the acts in a day the character of an offering, which makes them veritable living prayer. It is presumed, of course, that the will then remains in an attitude of giving, which will be subjacent, as it were, to the entire day. Whence the importance of the spirit of self-immolation in making our lives as a whole a veritable prayer.

Our lives can also be a prayer if, on all occasions, we keep our liberty of soul, the primary condition for prayer; for we thus remain in a constant state of availability for prayer. The necessity of inner self-discipline is again apparent here, since liberty of soul is synonymous with detachment from all creatures and all activity. But we shall have to learn to keep ourselves free in this way, while remaining capable of giving ourselves to our work and to our friends and comrades and brothers with gladness and natural simplicity. How far we have succeeded in keeping our freedom—which I would also call "inner silence"—will immediately become apparent when we begin to pray at our usual times; and it is love of Jesus' Cross which will enable us to keep it.

You will all feel, however, that this is not enough and that something more is necessary: practising this "diffused prayer." This will consist in placing short instants of prayer, at fairly frequent intervals, the length of your day. In other words, learn to pray either with the help of words or simply with a look of the soul, wherever you are, and also each time God incites you with His grace to do so; all with the utmost simplicity. It would be difficult for me to be any more explicit here, as no two of you will practise this "standing"—or, if you prefer, "permanent"—prayer in the same manner. It will take on as many different forms with you as there are differences between your natures and between your stages of development in faith. It may be a matter, say, of remembering a verse out of the Gospel or glancing towards Christ or feeling the presence of the Blessed Virgin, or it may be a matter of an intimate desire to make an offering for a comrade or for the whole of mankind, aroused by a friendly contact, by the sight of evil or by your being struck by the indifference of the crowd. In short, it is all a question of how one's faith reacts in becoming little by little regularly active as it should, and making one look towards the invisible realities of the world behind appearances. Such intermittent acts of faith, I must add, prepare the way for the state of contemplation which the gifts of the Holy Spirit can alone bring about in one.

Consciousness of being men's delegates before God, and more particularly of those with whom you come in contact—your mates at your work, the people living in the same village or the neighbors in your town or city—will be a very great help to you in acquiring this spirit, this vision of the world. You must work at it until it fixes itself in you, becomes part of you.

We are all mutually dependent, due to the bonds of the Mystical Body of Jesus. This is a fact which affects all men in the state of divine adoption, but it concerns us Little Brothers in a special way, first, on account of a special intention included by Jesus in His call to us and, secondly, because, in answering His call, we have made Him, in accordance with that special intention, an explicit offering of our desire to be a ransom for our fellow men. Definitive form, as well as official consecration by the Church, is given this answer of ours by adding to our perpetual profession, as we do, an act by which we abandon ourselves to God.

Our daily contact with men must contribute towards developing in us the sense of this spiritual solidarity. The bonds created by friendship, by companionship with those with whom we work, by the help we can lend in time of need are the image of an immensely deeper and more effective kind of assistance. Through these visible manifestations of unity, we must exercise ourselves at perceiving, with the eyes of faith, the invisible bonds which cause us to participate in the suffering and sin and misery and needs of other men, and more particularly of those who come closest to us.

As I have already suggested elsewhere, you must not let the too great measure of the suffering and evil you will see instil feelings of revolt or bitterness in you. Turn, rather, with all your faith, to the mystery of Jesus' suffering. Whatever your dismay, however great your temptations to despair, the mystery of

Jesus' suffering will, in every case, be the answer, the one answer—God's own silent answer—which will enable you to accept the mystery of suffering with hope. So accept the world's suffering, bear the world's suffering as Jesus bore it; bear it with Him, bear it in Him, with humility, gentleness and love.

While your vision of the invisible world will make strangers of you in the way I have already mentioned, it must not make you distant or indifferent. On the contrary, you should actually be more alive to those around you, precisely on account of what your faith and love enable you to reach in them. There are, however, two possible deviations to be avoided in connection with your presence to the suffering of others, and each of you will be exposed to one or the other of these according to his temperament. Some of you will have difficulty in coming out of your "ivory tower," due to shyness or some other trait of character or to the way you have been raised, or, again, on account of mistaken ideas regarding the conditions upon which union with God depends; but neither can there be any question—and this is the second of the two deviations I refer to—of letting yourselves off cheap with your prayer-life by striking a bargain between the time you devote to your contacts and the time you give to prayer. There will, of course, have to be something in the nature of a continual compromise here, because there are just so many hours in a day; but this is something different. What I mean is that this cutting-up of your time, this sort of competition for your time, must not be allowed to repeat itself inside you and put you off balance. To allow yourselves to think of your lives as made up of hours of retirement during which you are worshippers and hours of work or contacts during which you are something else, would be a grave mistake. The degree of your union with God will not be measured by the number of hours you devote to prayer each day, nor will you be men of prayer only insofar as these make you so. You will be men of prayer if and when your faith has made your way of looking at things and people like that of Jesus. The environment you live in will probably be one entirely bathed in the temporal, where aspirations towards greater justice and well-being and progress are confined within purely worldly perspectives. Watch out for contamination; keep your gaze trained on Jesus, and keep it clear and limpid. Remember always that it is for Him that you exist, for Him that you live, for Him that you are ready to give your lives for your fellow men.

There is another kind of evil the importance, and even the prevailing presence, of which may escape you unless you take care. I mean moral evil and sin and all the different kinds of moral evil and sin, including rejection of God. The sense of sin has been practically extinguished today in many people's consciences. Moral evil is too often gauged solely by its consequences in the economic sphere. Take care to keep the sense of sin well alive in you—that of the sin in yourselves as well as in the world and in every human being in it. If you have the sense of God in you;

if, above all, you have penetrated into the mystery of the Heart of Jesus, and if you live in intimacy with Him, you cannot help but experience His agony before the sins of all mankind; and, out of love for Him and out of love for men, your prayer will of itself become supplication and atonement.

Before leaving this subject of the development of your spiritual solidarity with mankind, I must say a word more about something you should always keep in mind. There can be no fertility except in union with Christ the Redeemer. Our solidarity with other men can therefore only be a consequence of our union with Christ. Watch out for any sign of a wedge here or anything that might break your inner balance; you can only be "saviors with Jesus" if you are saved by Him first. It is not for you, but rather for those so designated, to work to rebuild society and correct injustice and remove suffering. Your role is to belong solely and totally to Jesus, so as to enable Him to be present to your fellow men. There is a knowledge of Christ which can only reach men through the lives of those who love Him.

May I now have brought you to see how important, how irreplaceable the right kind of faith is going to be to you if you really wish to be "standing delegates to prayer." Let it be simple and straightforward, confident, untiringly persevering, staunch in moments of darkness, solidly and concretely fastened upon our Lord. It is our Lord Himself that your faith must take hold of, both through the Gospel and in

the reality of His presence at your side. Exercise your
faith tirelessly. Read the Gospel and see what Jesus
has to tell you about it. He hardly spoke of anything
else and He dwelt upon it so because He knew we
might not listen attentively enough, because He knew
we would get discouraged, because He knew we
would be lacking in perseverance. He knew only too
well that faith was the essence of it all! The words
He chose to tell us so, nothing can replace. So read
them; read them over and over again. But, above all,
live by them. "How is it that you call me, Master,
Master, and will not do what I bid you?" (Luke
6:46).

Do not go losing yourselves in your imaginations
or in devious, roundabout and unnecessarily confusing searchings. Jesus is there within your reach, if you
have faith. Nothing is more concrete, more tangible,
more true than faith, because it does just that—it
touches that constantly present Reality. *Jesus* is
present, and *you* will be present if you make yourselves alive to the passing moment. Your joys and
your woes, your fatigue from your work, your weariness of people, your dislikes and revulsions and your
pains—all these are but surface motion and can never
stop Jesus from being at your side, from loving you,
from wishing you closer to Him through the very
things that make you suffer, as an offering to His
Father and a sacrifice for your brother men. This is
reality, and the rest, in comparison, is nothing but
appearances.

Yes, I know, all this is easier said than done. But you must not forget that the Spirit of Light and of Love is at work in you. You must untiringly keep the way open for Him by the constant exercise of your faith in Jesus. The great temptation with prayer is lassitude. Look up what Jesus says about it in the Gospel, where He draws a meaningful contrast, not just with perseverance, but with "shameless asking" (Luke 11:8). It is thus that you will become our Lord's "standing delegates to prayer." "Listen, you that have ears to hear with" (Matthew 11:15). "What is impossible to man's powers is possible to God" (Luke 18:27). ". . . to him who believes, everything is possible" (Mark 9:23).

CHAPTER

7

"UNIVERSAL BROTHERS"

Father de Foucauld wanted his Brothers to be "universal brothers." Now, as I see you grow in age and numbers, I fear for you. I fear as I see your generous enthusiasm; as I see you feeling so deeply, so acutely the unjust and undeserved sufferings of the workers and the other poor; as I see you starting out to live and work among peoples who are looked down upon because of their race or because they have not evolved like us Westerners; as I see you approaching different kinds of civilizations, alive with anticipation, eager to understand them. I fear lest you succumb to the temptations by which the true kind of love is always ·assailed; I fear you may become hardened towards certain sorts of men or give in to impatience or lassitude. For, after all, you have your limitations and your prejudices, like everyone else.

There are few people on earth who know how to love like Jesus, and you are going to be lost in the world we live in today, which is more than ever a

world of hatred and division. You have the race
hatreds and racial oppositions, aggravated moreover
in certain places by the abuses of colonialism. On the
social plane, you have the oppositions between the
working classes and the proletariat and the richer
elements, constantly kept stimulated under the
principle of the class struggle. On the international
plane, you have the national rivalries and jealousies
and susceptibilities. And on the plane of religion
itself, you have all the schisms and forms of fanati-
cism and antisemitism, not to mention the lack of
understanding among the different rites within the
Church.

Living among the poor, as you come to share more
and more completely the conditions under which
they are obliged to live, you will feel in a new way,
as if in your own flesh, the wrongness of their lot
while too many Christians with satisfied souls go on
living in peace and quiet opposite them. There will
be times when you will wonder how anyone could
help feeling anger and an impulse to revolt against
those who have such an easy time of it in life. Since
we have chosen to march towards Christ by the road
of the poor, with no more of the essential means at
our disposal than theirs, why not then go through
with it and likewise take upon us a share in the
workers' struggle for justice? Are we yielding to an
obstinate hankering after rest and quiet to pray in?
Are we, then, afraid of so difficult a road?

No. Our refusal to take any active, or better, "responsible," part in the struggle of the workers in

quest of a better world is not dictated by any more
or less artificial "ideal" of the religious life, nor yet
by any pretense at representing the Church in some
special capacity. It is simply necessitated by the fact
of our belonging to the workers, as an indispensable
contribution to their struggle so that the struggle may
remain, or become, in effect, a Christian struggle.

Like all warfare, the struggle of the poor, however
just it may be both as regards its cause and as regards
its purpose, is nevertheless a blot on mankind. What
kind of ultimate conquest is it to be the instrument
to? What spirit should it therefore be led in? For
Christianity demands here that one shall constantly
watch and rectify one's acts. Now, the class struggle,
tending as it does towards harshness in human relations, can only replace one kind of oppression with
another, by its own weight, so to speak, unless it is
courageously controlled by love; and it is something
difficult indeed to make a struggle effectual without
hatred in the heart of the combatant. Yet love cannot
be engendered by hate. The great danger with even
the mildest form of warfare is that the human climate
it creates is favorable to new hatreds and fresh conflicts. The class struggle is no exception to this law.
In the thick of the battle, even, Christians must aim
at the establishment of a really human regime which
will make it possible for men to be united by love.
Nor is this by any means utopian. However great
the improbability that relations of this character
could be brought about at present, or for some time
to come, it is our inescapable duty to bend our efforts

in that direction. We can hardly deny the demands of the duty of love and unity which has been placed upon mankind by Christ, simply because we know we cannot accomplish it in a single stroke. The perfection which Christ is asking of the Christian worker at the present time must not be minimized. His heart and spirit must inevitably undergo and sustain the painful, but fruitful, tension between the equal demands of justice and of charity.

It is right here that you Little Brothers can bring at least to those of your working mates whose duty it is to fight, the spiritual ferment which will enable them to fight like Christians. You can thus belong to them completely—and I would go so far as to say that there can be no such thing as a Christian struggle for the workers unless the struggle does, in fact, carry within it a leaven of unity and love stronger than the hatred. You must be your brother workers' Christian strength, the antidote to the poison that threatens their love of Christ at every turn. Difficult, yes, very difficult it is for a man to reconcile in his heart the sentiments he must needs have in a struggle which, though just, is nevertheless a thing of violence, and the love which Christ expects of him for those against whom he is obliged to battle. I believe that it is as difficult as it is for a rich man to be poor in spirit or for a camel to pass through the eye of a needle.

But here one must remember that Christ said, "Such things are impossible to man's powers, but not to God's" (Mark 10:27). The people of Christ could not be conceived of without voluntary poor men who make themselves poor out of love, so that those who possess may be as if not possessing. Neither could it get along without men who are called by Christ to chastity in voluntary celibacy, as those who marry need to be reminded that they ought to live with a view to a higher spiritual end. Likewise, Christ's people could not get along without those few of whom He asks that they take certain demands of love and unity more literally than other men, so that the poor may learn to stand up for their rights without hatred and without letting their hearts become hard; it is necessary, I mean, that a few "self-made poor" live, in their midst, silently, the gentleness and peace of the Beatitudes. "But I tell you that you should not offer resistance to injury; if a man strikes you on the right cheek, turn the other cheek also towards him; if he is ready to go to law with thee over thy coat, let him have it and thy cloak with it" (Matt. 5:39-41).

It would likewise be a mistake to regard these words either as an oratorical exaggeration or as applicable to everyone indiscriminately. It is proper, it is necessary, that men should struggle to gain their essential rights to a kind of life which shall be both human and Christian, but this can in no way affect the Lord's teachings as regards the unlimited demands of the precept of love. Like voluntary celibacy and the freely willed self-dispossession of worldly goods, an attitude of non-violence and unity and peace is inscribed in the call which Christ makes to some at least of those whom He wishes to send with

His Gospel message among the unjustly dealt with poor.

Nor will it be easy for you to live in a way which will make all this understandable to men who know from experience that none of their basic rights has ever been granted them without their having fought for it. The vocation of the Little Brother-worker is a very exacting one. There must be nothing in your way of acting or your way of talking that could make your working mates think that your non-participation is accountable for by fear of exertion or some spurious idea that you are "too good for that sort of thing." That would be far indeed from the proper idea of "non-efficacy." This particular aspect of the Little Brothers' vocation does not, of course, apply to certain situations in which they could be properly accused of complicity were they content to look on as silent spectators. To stand up against a particular case of flagrant injustice directly affecting one's immediate comrades is not at all the same thing as fighting for a change of social structures.

A similar but still more delicate situation which may arise for some of you is this. Those of you who are, or will be, working in countries under the regime of a colony or a protectorate or a mandate, may find the people engaging in either underground or openly violent action for an independence to which they justly aspire. You must then do your best to make those around you see that you believe in, and adhere inwardly in all loyalty, not to their action, but to their cause, over and beyond all nationalism. I realize how difficult this will be, because you will be obliged to reject particular forms of participation which they would normally regard as the only convincing proof you could give of your sincerity. It will sometimes happen, whatever you may do or say, that you are misunderstood by either side; yet you will have to bear the general reprobation, so as to keep intact the equal demands of justice and of universal love, which it is more particularly the mission of the Fraternities to incarnate among the peoples. This will often go very hard with you, and you will then have to cling with all your faith to your belief in the ultimate efficacy of lives sacrificed out of faithfulness to the unequivocal and unquestionable counsels which Christ has given mankind. Such faithfulness may, indeed, lead to your expulsion and the material ruin of your Fraternity; to your persecution, or perhaps even your imprisonment or death. Others before you have suffered the honor of being witnesses of the spirit of Jesus to the end, in the midst of a world incapable of receiving it.

The first temptation to which your love of your brother men is going to be exposed is, then, letting yourselves be drawn into closing your eyes to everything but the rights and aspirations of the poor, and forgetting that you must continue to love all men through and beyond their strife. "Why, what credit is it to you, if you love those who love you? Even sinners love those who love them" (Luke 6:32).

With the generosity and enthusiasm of your youth, many of you have answered a call to dedicate your lives to peoples differing completely from us as to mentality, culture and level of development. After the usual first period of newness and discovery, the reality of things may have turned out to be, not precisely disappointing, but other than what you had anticipated. It may also be that you had somewhat minimized the difficulties, or oversimplified the problem.

The friendship you came to bring these peoples in all openness and frankness may not have been understood; may in fact have aroused suspicion. For you belong, you must remember, to different races; you belong sometimes to nations by which they have been conquered; you may belong to those peoples whose technological civilization seems to them, from experience, to be destructive of certain of their secular values, both human and national. In witness of your desire to give yourselves to them completely—as well as by way of giving concrete form to the offering which, as Little Brothers, you have made of yourselves in a spirit of redemption—it was your wish to be able to share as far as you could the conditions under which they live, to do the same kinds of work as they, to speak their language, etc., but you may have quickly come to realize that you were not going to be able to achieve this either as easily or as completely as you had hoped. You may have found yourselves prevented from doing so by lack of physical adaptation, difficulty in accustoming yourselves to the food, inability to pronounce the language correctly or even to retain it in your memories. Something you may find still more disturbing is perhaps their reticence towards you; even those you feel warmest towards never seem to forget that you are foreigners, foreigners, indeed, as if in every fibre of your respective beings. They make you feel this in their attitude towards you at every turn. In a word, they have not adopted you as the love with which you went to them had made you think they would do.

Nor is this all. Whether you will or not, you have been made and fashioned by generations of ancestors, and your minds, your whole mental and moral complexion have once for all been marked by the environment from which you have come. Your reactions and your appreciations are not only different but sometimes actually the opposite to theirs. Your decision to dedicate yourself to these people for whom God has given you a profound and, as it were, natural liking has brought about no change in your deeper, instinctive psychological constitution. It would have seemed to you that this liking would always make you see everything about them in a favorable light, but once your first impressions have worn off, this has not always proven to be the case. In fact, you may no longer feel attracted to them in quite the same way; the pull which you felt in the beginning may have lessened under the friction of the everyday contact or the irritation produced by the constantly disagreeing views about so many different things, perhaps even under veritable clashes of sensibilities or temperaments.

You, of course, continue to love them with all your faith in your vocation and you mean to remain

staunch in your self-giving. There can be no question
of your wishing either to retire or to withdraw any
part of what you have given. But it pains you to find
yourselves no different, to find your hurts, your moments of inner weariness, your moments of impatience, your disgust at certain habits and customs,
perhaps even your bursts of anger, betraying in you
the creature of your particular country and your particular kind of civilization. All this may burden you,
and burden you heavily. There may be times when
you are no longer quite sure on just which side the
true values lie. Try as you may, the pain of remaining strangers in the midst of peoples you are meant
to love may grow sharper and harder to bear. You
will then be ripe for a serious temptation, either to
give up trying to understand them at all or to judge
them with unjust severity. If, despite the differences
between you, they could only come to realize in the
end that you love them like brothers, with no feeling
of superiority either of race or ability towards them,
none of all this would matter. But this will not always
happen, and you may have to resign yourselves to
finishing your lives among them without having succeeded in convincing them that you came to them
simply as friends and brothers. All your contentment
will then have to be confined to knowing that you
have been silently followed, all the way through, by
God and that, however dimly to you, He will have
approved your generosity and ratified your sacrifice.

The state of things which I have just been describ-
ing will have prepared you for succumbing to the il-

lusions of some substitute for love, especially when, due to physical fatigue or reduced vitality and nervous tension, you begin to wish—oh, how naturally!—that you were back in the familiar surroundings of your own country. There are times in life when a man's whole bulwark of virtues seems to crumble, as if all the powers of the will sustaining it had suddenly given out. When this happens to you you will find yourselves confronted with the supreme test of love, for you will have gone as far as your possibilities allowed you to go and, in the souls of you, now stripped and naked before God, there will be no alternative to opening up your weakness to love of another's making—love of the making of the heart of Jesus—and becoming but its instrument, abandoned to Him at last in faith.

Meanwhile, your temptation will be to conclude that, at bottom, you are "just like the next man"—for instance, those other "Whites" in your vicinity who may have been observing your attempts to love your African or Arab or Indian brothers, with a smile of indulgence—and to let it go at that.

Little Brothers, let me warn you that this is a very serious temptation, one, indeed, which would strike at our very purpose in going among these poor that are so despised, on the one hand, and treated with such high-minded, pitying indulgence, on the other. I only hope that, by knowing beforehand what difficulties to expect, you will be able to handle them the better. One of the gravest of these is that you are, or will be, in contact with persons of good will and earnest intelligence, knowing the country and the people better than you (and these will sometimes be missionaries or religious of either sex), who will try to convince you, out of their own, and often long, experience, that you are making a mistake in attempting to deal with "the natives" on a footing of fraternal equality. I am not speaking here of certain kinds of civil servants or trades people or colonials who make no effort at all to hide their feeling of superiority, brutal as it sometimes is, or who are merely out for their own interests or those of the business they represent. Their attitude, on the contrary, will give you a healthy reaction. I am speaking, rather, of those who, while loving and devoting themselves to the people, even to the point of exhausting their strength for them, do so nevertheless with a certain consciousness of superiority. I beg of you, do not believe that you will ever know how to love as you should so long as the slightest sentiment like this has any place in you. Jesus has not bidden us *just to have pity* on men to whom we consider ourselves superior because of our superior civilization; He has bidden us to *love them like brothers*, and this is a very different matter.

They will tell you how backward, how undeveloped, how like children these people are in so many ways, and how we must make ourselves their educators and consequently use firmness and severity with them "for their own good." The problem, I fear, is one of great, great delicacy, and I doubt whether it is possible to settle it either quite so definitively or quite so easily. I am obviously lacking in great experience and I know these peoples much less well than those who have spent a good part of their lives in their midst. I have, however, lived for more than fifteen years among the Arabs, mixing more closely with them than many a civil servant or colonial, and I have thus perhaps acquired at least a certain degree of experience. Yet, I wish simply to echo what our Lord would say to us, were He to come today to teach us the precept of brotherly love. No one has ever known better than He what is at the bottom of the human heart. "He . . . did not need assurances about any man, because he could read men's hearts" (John 2:25). But, even for the very littlest of men, He never had the shadow of a sentiment resembling the pity of the strong or the just or the wise for the weak and the sinner and the ignorant; He *loved us*— and what a respectful love for each He loved us with! How, then, could it be our right to entertain towards our brothers in weakness and ignorance—in human nature, in short—any sentiment which the *Son of Man* would not consider it permissible for Him to entertain towards us? We shall be dealt with by Him as we shall have dealt with others; be judged by Him as we shall have judged others—all others. Respect, esteem, patience in understanding and the total absence of all desire to judge or condemn are essential ingredients of love. See to it that you do not abdicate before these demands; or rather, whenever your human strength gives out and argument fails you also, just look towards Christ and, opening up those hearts of yours thus emptied of yourselves, let Him put there a power to love other than your own.

Are we to be firm, severe, exacting, because it is a duty for us to educate? Yes, perhaps—but on two conditions: first, that it is actually our business, and therefore our right, to educate; secondly, that we do so without the slightest trace of contempt or superiority. Do not then judge by reference to your own scale of moral values, but rather by comparison with the divine values, and these alone. Only God has a right to judge by comparison with self; He alone sees to the bottom of men's hearts. It is not our affair to gauge men's worth on their ability or inability to adapt themselves to our ways of thinking, to our ways of working, to our habits of cleanliness and principles of hygiene or our codes of good manners and social conduct. They may annoy, they may make us suffer because they are different from us in these respects; it does not necessarily follow that they are not quite as much men or men any less good than we.

Neither does our role as Little Brothers include working for their adaptation to the Western materialistic, technological form of civilization, which, moreover, comes far from representing the only conceivable idea of a really human civilization. I do not deny, as I have said before, that the technical ability which has given man of the West so great a domination over nature is, in itself, a form of human progress, or that there is no way of preventing it either from increasing in momentum or from spreading; but

I cannot take up here the extremely delicate question as to how possible it is for peoples still at a low level of development, whose social structure is purely of the pre-machine description, to be brought with any degree of rapidity into our cycle of civilization without injury to their psychological and moral balance. The weight which materialism-working technology puts upon man is such, if he is not to be crushed or debased by it, as necessarily to presuppose that he possesses a maturity and a spiritual strength which can only come from Christianity actually lived with all its demands of detachment and selflessness. My purpose in bringing up the point here has simply been to stress the attitude of mind and soul which has been made compulsory upon us by Christ's first commandment, whatever the task of educating those who may be placed in our care may be.

It behooves us to remember as well that the violent, sometimes passionate, reactions which we criticize certain populations for so severely—ill temper, obstinacy, laziness, disloyalty, etc.—deplorable as they may be, are often merely reflexes of self-defense against the brutal or high-handed manner of too many Europeans. It is therefore we Europeans who are really responsible for this sort of thing, and we would do better to direct our criticisms towards ourselves.

I also feel constrained to repeat here what I have said to you on other occasions as regards working with these people when the job demands any degree of technical proficiency, say, for example, building or machine-repairing. You must watch yourselves especially carefully here. It is beyond these men, in their present state of development, to be the kind of helpers you would like—and their inability, you may be sure, has no moral importance in the eyes of God. Rather than lose your sense of judgment or fairness with them, I would say that it would be better for you to be prepared to have them make a botch of, or even spoil, a piece of work too difficult for them. The nomads of the high plateaux of Algeria or the primitive colored people in the mountains of the Cameroons, who have succeeded through the centuries in forging human groups which can cope with the most ungrateful soil with the simplest of tools and methods, and survive on so very little, are men in the full sense of the term—sometimes more than we in certain respects.

When I saw the gigantic, awe-inspiring feats of the Incas on the steep slopes of the valleys of the Cordilleras—the terraces they built for their agriculture, the waterways they cut out of the rock for irrigation, etc.—I could not help thinking that the tremendous struggle for life which these obviously denote must have fashioned a type of man somewhat stronger and more wholesome than many a tourist of today stepping from luxurious cars to contemplate those ruins with an air of unthinking superiority. The motor car is undoubtedly a victory of the human mind, and one can but bow to technology before such a thing of progress; but the mind is not the whole of

man and we moderns are too inclined to forget it.
Ah, if we could only see man as Christ sees him!

But that, in fact, is precisely what we must try to
do; we must strive, in faith, to couple our regard
upon mankind to God's. If we are attentive enough
to so necessary a purpose, we shall be preserved from
the kind of judgment which otherwise, I fear, will too
often be that of the Pharisee. Are we to judge the
poor, those who so lack man-made means, those who
have nothing? How, then, can we tell whether they
are not better men than we, whether they are not
closer than we to God? It would really be a very good
thing if we could stop confusing scientific and technical values with human and moral superiority.

As far as we Little Brothers are concerned, the one
thing we possess the value of which is certainly
superior, is the deposit of Revelation and the message
of the Gospel. They do not belong to us, either; they
are not ours to keep: we must give them to these peoples, with the conviction deep in our hearts that the
only way we have learnt to live them is like Pharisees
and Doctors of the Law.

I may be stressing all this unnecessarily, for you
will feel most of it yourselves, if you have not already done so. There is still another point, however,
on which I wish to give you better warning. After the
temptation of setting yourselves up as judges and
educators, you will probably experience a temptation
to take refuge in kind-hearted pity, which is another

way of refusing to respect and esteem human beings
and evading the commandment of fraternal love.
Wearying of having constantly to react against the
ambient attitude of disfavor and censure among the
"Whites," you may be tempted to think that you are
simply persisting in an erroneous opinion and that,
precisely because these peoples are "rightly" despised, and consequently the most forsaken of all, the
best way you can love them is to put yourselves on
their level, make yourselves one with them in the
general contempt, and share their sufferings in silence. But this again would be wrong, an abdication
of love. One can, of course, throw oneself into suffering of this kind; that is not what I mean; I mean that
in Jesus' way of taking human weakness upon Him,
there was something more than just pity. You would
therefore have no right to limit your feeling for these
brothers of yours thus, whatever their race and whatever their place in the human scale. You most certainly must make yourselves one with them; I make
bold to say, though, that you must do so with a certain pride at being their brothers. If it were given us
to see inside their hearts and understand them as they
actually are with the life they have, and then to com-
pare what we would probably be like if we had had
to be born and grow up and live under the same conditions, I think we should feel quite small beside
them—and be considerably more reserved in our judgments. This is no matter of ready-made sentiment,
you may be certain; it is one of true humility which

we can only obtain from the light of the Divine Presence in us.

The primary requisite to authentic universal fraternal love is indeed that one shall have become capable of seeing oneself with humility.

To speak of universal fraternal love is to speak of unity. The Little Brothers must therefore learn, first of all, to live such unity within the Fraternities.

Now, our unity will not be simply the result of fraternal affection uniting us in a common ideal. Authentic as is that mode of Christ's presence among us, mutual love, there is another factor making for our unity, and that is obedience, the *mystery of obedience* in each of our souls. We are meant to be an organically conceived body, whose head is Jesus. Our unity will consequently come from a fraternal fusion in charity on the horizontal plane and from a simultaneous converging on the vertical towards Christ, mysteriously present not only among us, but in the humblest brother in charge of the smallest Fraternity, who must therefore be obeyed.

This mystery of obedience, making as it will both the strength of our unity and the realistic firmness of our love of and attachment to Christ, is essential to the fullness of our life together. Setting up a Fraternity is no mere matter of having brothers live together, however deeply united they may be in selfless friendship, but one of their becoming, as I say, an organic body made alive by its head, Christ. It can only be through the complete truthfulness of our adherence to Christ which obedience means, that such organic unity will come about in the Fraternities and have the effects it must have on our charity, our poverty, and renunciation, as also on our work.

But there is a stubborn obstacle to our requisite transparency, and therefore to our unity, an obstacle too often met with, too familiar to too many of us: our congenital—and almost inexplicable—insistence upon seeing everything from our own point of view and judging with our temperaments, our personal likes and dislikes and our partialities; in other words, the small view we take of things and the ever repeated narrowness of our judgments. There are many causes for this upon which we must act simultaneously, causes such as lack of instinctive undertaking, lack of natural breadth of mind, inborn prejudice, inexperience of life and of people, self-conceit.

All this would be considerably attenuated if we could see the presumption at the root of many of our sententious judgments and statements of position, which are so destructive of unity, wounding to love, stifling to joy, and which only make us the more inaccessible to Christ and the less open to our fellow men.

So become aware of your insufficiencies and limitations. Do not waste yourselves in sterile discussions either on points of detail or on false problems or on matters of which you know too little. Do not judge inconsiderately, either, but make yourselves capable of giving everyone, whoever he is—and therefore even more so, if anything, one of your own brothers in a Fraternity—the benefit of the doubt integral to fraternal love when it is properly humble.

I cannot finish this letter without having pointed to a further danger, one which the Congregation itself is beginning to run in this same respect, owing to the appearance among us of vocations originating with men of different countries and different races.

Like any new departure, the Little Brothers of Jesus had to have some place to start in, and this happens to have been France. It was with French Brothers that the Congregation learned to walk, if I may say so, and it was with French Brothers that its ideal was long meditated upon, experimented with, and finally worked out. But it was always meant to be universal; in other words, it must be capable of being in all countries and for all nations what it has become among the people of France.

For some time now, Brothers have been coming from different places as well as from France, and this is a source of great joy and encouragement both for the individual Fraternities and for the Congregation as a whole. On the other hand—and you must all be thoroughly aware of this—it is the start of a critical turning-point in our growth, and one which may well put the entire undertaking to the test both as regards its openness and as regards its unity. We Frenchmen have some very bad faults. One of these is a certain superficial quickness in our judgments of other countries and peoples, coupled with a propen-

sity to judge from our own standards and as if France
held the unique privilege of some absolute and uni-
versally applicable conception of what civilization is.
The Brothers who come from elsewhere will, of
course, feel this more than those who are French and
they will consequently be tempted to hold back before throwing themselves wholeheartedly into the
Fraternity as they find it, and to try first to differenti-
ate between what appeals to them as universal in the
way we operate and what may be specifically French.

A task of purification like this, necessary as it may
be, requires a kind of experience and a degree of self-
detachment which none of you can have yet acquired
and, if those who are not French were to insist upon
rejecting that which they thought too purely French,
they would be running the risk of remaining more at-
tached than they should to their national prejudices;
for we all have them. You all know how greatly I desire to have the Fraternities really adapt themselves
in each country where they are established. But there
is another, and a still higher and purer, kind of witness for us to give, that of perfect unity exemplified
through the requisite measure of renunciation with
regard to our respective national casts of thought. At
a time like this when, despite widespread, anxious
gropings towards international unity, national prejudices seem to have become more violent and more
conflicting than ever, it certainly does not behoove
us to go about our problem of adaptation by emphasizing our differences, but rather to diminish our differences by seeking unity over and beyond our

national temperaments, through the very suffering, and the consequent possibilities of self-detachment, which those differences bring. If anything has to be risked or sacrificed, it had better be a bit of our national individualities rather than any part of the existing deep fraternal unity; for that unity cannot continue to build unless we relinquish personal views as to what the Congregation and the individual Fraternities should be like. I ask you all—those who come from France and those who have joined us from elsewhere—to make this effort.

I cannot yet tell how, later on, once the Fraternities have spread far enough abroad to have earned the name "universal," the fraternal unity which must keep us all knit together in mutual affection and respect for one another's diversities, is to express itself. Our diversities, in any event, will be no obstacle to that unity, if our fraternal love is humble, simple and selfless enough to make them like the language of the soul when it speaks spontaneously to God in its own individual way. Unless the simplicity and selflessness goes deep enough, however, the brothers will not succeed in attaining the unity for which Christ prayed before His agony.

If you allow yourselves to follow your over-instinctive reactions, and fail to submit to the laws of love and to open your hearts to the solicitations of Christ crucified, the Fraternities will inevitably be drawn towards division by their own weight. Here, I know, I need only appeal to your own experience within the Congregation. You certainly realize that it is precisely because we need and mean to go all the way through to unity among us, in complete openness to one another, that we suffer more from the differences between us than we otherwise should—those differences, I mean, for which our original environments, our upbringing and our individual temperaments are responsible. It is a gift from God to have been called together from so many different places. Wherever you come from, you all have something to learn from each other; you must therefore strive to know one another by getting away from your own angles of vision and placing yourselves at those of the others; and, in order to do this, you must raise yourselves above personal feelings.

Suffer from one another you will—I am afraid that is inevitable. But it will help you to love one another without illusion. It will also preserve you from the temptation of confining your love to one class of people or one single nation.

You will thus learn to regard each man with what I might call "preconceived liking," and your hearts will stay young and your minds open and understanding. Over and beyond all your differences, keep courageously, perseveringly, on this path of openness and mutual self-giving. Never let yourselves close up inside out of a faint heart or a weary mind. The way will sometimes be hard, but it will put your minds and hearts in that propitious state which will enable the Lord to choose and use them for a living expression of His love among men.